Wounded Knee Massacre

Wounded Knee Massacre

Martin Gitlin

Landmarks of the American Mosaic

GREENWOOD

AN IMPRINT OF ABC-CLIO, LLC
Santa Barbara, California • Denver, Colorado • Oxford, England

Library of Congress Cataloging-in-Publication Data

Gitlin, Martin
  Wounded Knee Massacre / Martin Gitlin.
    p. cm. — (Landmarks of the American mosaic)
  Includes bibliographical references and index.
    ISBN 978-1-59884-409-2 (hard copy : alk. paper)—ISBN 978-1-59884-410-8 (ebook) 1. Wounded Knee Massacre, S.D., 1890—Juvenile literature. I. Title.
  E83.89.G58   2011
  973.8′6—dc22   2010035200

ISBN: 978-1-59884-409-2
EISBN: 978-1-59884-410-8

15 14 13 12 11   1 2 3 4 5

This book is also available on the World Wide Web as an eBook. Visit www.abc-clio.com for details.

ABC-CLIO, LLC
130 Cremona Drive, P.O. Box 1911
Santa Barbara, California 93116-1911

This book is printed on acid-free paper ∞

Manufactured in the United States of America

This book is dedicated to my brother, Bobby,
whose fascination with the American Indian
in his youth and beyond piqued my interest
in the subject and who continues to be an
inspiration to me in my professional endeavors today.

Contents

Series Foreword

THE LANDMARKS OF THE AMERICAN MOSAIC series comprises individual volumes devoted to exploring an event or development central to this country's multicultural heritage. The topics illuminate the struggles and triumphs of American Indians, African Americans, Latinos, and Asian Americans, from European contact through the turbulent last half of the twentieth century. The series covers landmark court cases, laws, government programs, civil rights infringements, riots, battles, movements, and more. Written by historians especially for high school students on up and general readers, these content-rich references satisfy more thorough research needs and provide a deeper understanding of material that students might only otherwise be exposed to in a short section in a textbook or superficial explanation online.

Each book on a particular topic is a one-stop reference source. The series format includes

- Introduction
- Chronology
- Narrative chapters that trace the evolution of the event or topic chronologically
- Biographical profiles of key figures
- Selection of crucial primary documents
- Glossary
- Bibliography
- Index

This landmark series promotes respect for cultural diversity and supports the social studies curriculum by helping students understand multicultural American history.

Preface

THE PASSAGE OF TIME tends to bring specific moments in history into greater focus, even after all who experienced them have passed on. In fact, the loss of all those who can bring first-hand accounts can often result in greater objectivity and clarity to a particular event.

But one can't discount the critical need for sources imparting the views of people who played a role or at least witnessed a historic episode. The importance of the availability of varying accounts, especially in the authoring of a book about an emotional and heatedly debated topic such as the Wounded Knee massacre, can't be minimized.

Many students reading this will be learning about the tragedy that occurred on December 29, 1890, for the first time. The purpose here is to provide an as objective and informative book as possible, making it ideal as reference material for students.

The *Wounded Knee Massacre* highlights the entire scope of the relationship between white settlers, the United States government, and the Plains Indians throughout the eighteenth and nineteenth century, with a focus on the events from the 1860s until that bloody morning in snowy South Dakota.

The heart of the book is organized chronologically, as is the Primary Documents section, which provides first-hand accounts of events leading up to, including, and following the Wounded Knee massacre.

The book also features a number of ready-reference materials, including a timeline of important events leading up to and including the Wounded Knee tragedy, biographies of key figures in the relationship between the Indians and the U.S. military, and a glossary that offers readers a knowledge of Sioux terminology.

Introduction

As late as the 1830s the Plains Indians lived happily in their element. One can't claim they existed peacefully; they both raided and were victims of raids, resulting in battles with tribes such as the Crow, leaving many dead. But their way of life remained uninterrupted. Roaming thousands of square miles around them were millions of buffalo on which they depended for food, clothing, goods, and even shelter. They had come into contact with the white man, but only as traders they deemed beneficial to their ability to thrive.

At the time whites populated the area far east of the Mississippi River almost exclusively. They eventually succumbed to a desire to explore and inhabit the vast expanses west. They were motivated not only by curiosity and the wide open spaces but also by reports of gold being discovered in California and elsewhere. The U.S. government supported the initiatives of white settlers and miners, bringing one and all into direct conflict with the Indians.

That conflict was inevitable, not merely because whites were destined to pass through Lakota territory but also due to a distinct clash of cultures and priorities. Both white people and the government that represented them were motivated by wealth and possessions. The capitalist system in America had been well established. But the Lakota didn't understand and they became angry and frustrated when whites with desires foreign to the Indian infringed on their way of life by trespassing on their lands, killing off the buffalo, and bringing diseases that began to kill off their people.

As conflicts ensued, many ordinary Americans and those in power clung to the growing belief in Manifest Destiny, which asserted the right and inevitability of whites to control the

North American continent. Though the term was coined in reference to the struggle to wrest Texas from Mexico, it also related
to the various Indian nations that populated America from coast
to coast. The most significant hurdle standing in the way of
westward expansion was the Lakota, which by the middle of the
nineteenth century had proven its dominance over the other
Plains tribes, though the Cheyenne certainly remained a force.
The theory of Manifest Destiny contended that Divine Providence gave the white Christian man the right to take over land
inhabited by perceived inferiors. And the "red savages" populat-
ing the Plains certainly fell into that category.

There was no blueprint for the process of subduing the
Lakota. The motivations of white expansionists and their government contrasting with those of the Plains Indians made conflict inevitable, particularly considering that the greed of many
whites resulted in the breaking of treaties signed by both parties. And the huge numbers of whites, in addition to their tech-
nological and military advantage, made the result of the Indian
wars a foregone conclusion.

There were some Indian victories along the way, most notably
the destruction of General George Custer and his Seventh Cavalry in the Battle of the Little Bighorn in 1876. But such triumphs merely served to hasten their own demise due to white
backlash that strengthened and prioritized government resolve
either to kill off the Indians or place them securely on reservations that grew smaller and smaller as the nineteenth century
marched on.

Indian leadership deteriorated and the Sioux no longer
enjoyed strength in numbers following Little Bighorn. Sitting
Bull and his band retreated to Canada. Crazy Horse was killed
in a defiant stand as he turned himself in to the agency. Other
chiefs had adopted life on a reservation, Christianity, farming,
and schooling for their children. Thousands of their people followed suit.

Most Americans, including those in power, didn't understand
those among the dwindling number of Indians who remained
determined to shun the white way of life. They couldn't—or
wouldn't—tolerate or comprehend the values of Lakota

traditionalists who yearned to remain as free as their ancestors. It seemed that only the whites who fought for Indian rights sympathized with the plight of the Sioux living on reservations, where they were not provided with the essentials promised them, including food and land.

Starvation and disease ran rampant at what was formerly known as the Great Sioux Reservation, which had been shrunk markedly to make way for white settlers. Many Indians grew desperate and angry. Droughts in the late 1880s made farming impossible, particularly to those such as the Lakota that had such little experience tilling the land.

Many Indians had given up hope, so it should come as no surprise that those with a stronger sense of spirituality embraced the Ghost Dance. Though various interpretations of the Ghost Dance were born as its practice was passed down from Paiute religious leader Wovoka to various tribes, those who danced believed it would lead to salvation and freedom from white dominance. The Lakota were promised that their dead ancestors would spring to life, the wildlife would return to the Plains, and the whites would disappear, thereby giving the Indians an opportunity to thrive in the lifestyle they once embraced on the land they deemed not only sacred, but rightfully theirs.

It has been said that the resistance of Plains Indians was broken for the final time at Wounded Knee, but such claims are misleading. Resistance against the overwhelming might of the U.S. military had died soon after Little Bighorn. Neither the sporadic fighting thereafter nor the Ghost Dance could ever be interpreted as resistance. Though incidents of Lakota defiance dotted the historical landscape a few weeks before and after the Wounded Knee massacre, they served as no threat to their inevitable subjugation on reservations.

The problem was that white America, including the government, didn't know what to make of the strange dancing. Fear overcame reason and those who believed it was a prelude to violence decided to take action. Rather than allow the Ghost Dancing to die a natural death, particularly after the Lakota realized it was not having its intended effect, those frightened by it demanded it be ceased. One result was the attempted arrest of revered Hunkpapa chief Sitting Bull, which brought about a scuffle that ended in his death. More than any other single incident, that tragedy served as a prelude to Wounded Knee. It set off a chain of events that ultimately resulted in the massacre. It prompted Sitting Bull's followers to join others who escaped from the reservations to freely practice the Ghost Dance and prompted an overwhelming military response.

It would be foolhardy to claim that the final nail in the coffin of Lakota militancy was destined to be placed violently, as occurred at Wounded Knee, though it has been contended that the massacre was perpetrated by cavalrymen who sought revenge for the slaughter at Little Bighorn. The Indians were already greatly subdued. Even those at Wounded Knee were awaiting word for the trip back to the reservation to begin. And according to nearly everyone who bore witness to the event and survived, almost all their weapons had been confiscated.

Wounded Knee marked the worst slaughter of American Indians in the nation's history, a fact that is difficult to grasp when one considers that Lakota militancy barely existed by that winter morning of 1890. How their relationship with white America and its government deteriorated to the point in which a tragedy such as the massacre could occur is fascinating and, particularly one hundred twenty years later, mind-boggling. But one must return to the basic premise that the notion of white superiority and Manifest Destiny made the permanence of reservation life for the American Indian inevitable. The destruction of chief Big Foot and his followers at Wounded Knee was merely an exclamation point placed on the conclusion of the Indian wars of the nineteenth century.

Chronology of Native American-U.S. Government Relations, 1804–1891

1804   The Sioux come across the Lewis and Clark Expedition, setting off a period of cooperation and activity between the Lakota and white traders.

1825   The U.S. government signs a treaty with Oglala Sioux recognizing the sovereignty of the Lakota nation.

1834   Oglala leader Bull Bear moves his tribe close to the recently opened Fort William (later Fort Laramie) in western South Dakota, a center for trading activity.

1849   The United States purchases Fort Laramie and dispatches troops there.

1851   Lakota, Cheyenne, Arapaho, and other Plains tribes sign the first of a series of treaties that establish territorial boundaries and allow white passage through their territories in exchange for payments to the tribes. The Fort Laramie Treaty of 1851 clears the way for the influx of miners and wagon trains on the Oregon and later the Bozeman trails, though the flood of humanity doesn't begin until after the Civil War.

September 3, 1855   About thirteen hundred soldiers under the command of Colonel William Harvey slaughter an entire Brule village in response to the killing of thirty soldiers. The army contingent had been destroyed in retribution for the murder of Brule chief Conquering Bear in a dispute over a cow that had been stolen by an Indian brave.

1862   The enactment of the Homestead Act motivates a wave of white settlers to pour across the Plains.

August 18, 1862   Santee Sioux warriors embark on a murder-ous rampage in Minnesota after being denied food and supplies. More than one thousand white citizens are killed.

December 26, 1862   Though more than three hundred Santee are condemned to death, President Abraham Lincoln issues a wave of pardons which lowers the number executed for the kill-ings in Minnesota to thirty-eight. On this date the largest public execution in American history is held.

November 29, 1864   One-time Methodist minister Colonel John Chivington, who was running for the Congress partially on a platform of keeping Colorado citizens safe from Indian aggres-sion, leads a group of troops and volunteers to the Cheyenne camp led by Chief Black Kettle and massacres more than one hundred men, women, and children, horribly mutilating and rav-aging many of them. Chivington brags about his exploits and is embraced by Coloradans until details of the slaughter are pro-duced, after which he is reviled as a cold-blooded killer.

July 1865   Three columns of soldiers are organized by General Patrick Conner to begin an incursion into the Powder River Basin, from the Black Hills to the Big Horn Mountains. Their order is to kill every Indian aged twelve and over. Conner builds a fort on the Powder River while wagon trains start rolling across the area into the gold fields of Montana.

July 24–26, 1865   The Battle of Platte Bridge results in the kill-ing of a Cavalry platoon by Cheyenne and Lakota warriors. The troops had been dispatched to meet a wagon train.

August 29, 1865   Conner's troops kill about fifty Arapaho and ravage their village in what became known as the Battle of Tongue River.

Late September 1865   Cheyenne chief Roman Nose leads his warriors in an attack to avenge the Sand Creek Massacre. Sev-eral hundred warriors armed only with bows and arrows and a few old guns kill a few soldiers and drive the rest back to Fort Laramie.

October 14, 1865   Most of Colorado Territory is ceded to the U.S. government in a treaty signed by the Southern Cheyenne.

Late Fall 1865   The Brule, Hunkpapa, Oglala, and Miniconjou sign a series of treaties which the government touts as an ending to the war on the Plains, but the boast is premature, to say the least. Most of the chiefs don't sign.

June 13, 1866   What is known as Red Cloud's war launches when Colonel Henry Carrington and hundreds of soldiers reach Fort Laramie with plans to build a number of forts along the Bozeman Trail. Red Cloud and fellow Lakota and Cheyenne chiefs Spotted Tail, Standing Elk, and Dull Knife are convoked to Fort Laramie on this date to negotiate a treaty, but discover to their dismay and anger that the government already has every intention to build the forts whether an agreement is reached or not.

July 13, 1866   The construction of Fort Phil Kearny begins on the forks of the Little Piney and Big Piney Creeks in the heart of the most fertile Lakota hunting grounds. The Cheyenne start a policy of harassment of soldiers who leave the camp and are aided by other Plains Indian tribes such as the Lakota, Arapaho, and Crow.

December 21, 1866   Young and talented Oglala warrior Crazy Horse helps a contingent of warriors execute a complex and daring plan to draw soldiers out of Fort Phil Kearny, resulting in the death of a number of officers. Two thousand Indians camp two miles away and set up various trap locations while a small group of young warriors, including Crazy Horse, lure all eighty soldiers out of the fort. The hidden warriors then spring into action, killing all the men. Some Indians were killed by the new repeating rifles, but what became known by the whites as the Fetterman Massacre is clearly an Indian victory. Captain William Fetterman, who commanded the fort, had bragged that he could defeat the entire Sioux nation with those eighty men.

April 29, 1868   The Army agrees to abandon the forts along the Bozeman Trail, but the Fort Laramie Treaty creates the Great Sioux Reservation, which serves to restrict Indian freedom. The reservation, however, encompasses much of the area for hunting to which the Lakota had become accustomed, including the sacred Black Hills and vast lands in Montana and Wyoming Territories. The Treaty of 1868 is designed to keep white settlers off Indian lands.

June 16, 1870 Red Cloud concludes his trip to Washington and New York City with a speech to a sympathetic crowd in the latter. He plays upon the emotions of his listeners in describing the relationship between his Lakota and the U.S. government, but his words have little impact on future events.

1873 General George Custer arrives on the Northern Plains to guard those surveying for the Northern Pacific Railroad. His expedition to the Black Hills a year later uncovers gold and results in a flood of fortune seekers into the area in direct disregard to the Treaty of 1868. The government feigns interest in keeping the gold rushers out of the Black Hills before officially opening it up to mining in 1875. The Sioux, rebuff the government's attempt to purchase the Black Hills for six million dollars, and then the government declares that all Sioux not on the reservation by January 31, 1876, will be considered hostile and subject to arrest.

Spring 1876 The largest contingent of Plains Indians ever assembled gather in an encampment on the Little Bighorn River in Montana. An estimated seven thousand Sioux, Cheyenne, and Arapaho show unity and map out a strategy against white encroachment and military force.

June 17, 1876 In the Battle of Rosebud Creek, General George Crook and his men confront Sioux and Cheyenne warriors led by Oglala chief Sitting Bull and Crazy Horse. The attack plan by the Indians confounds Crook and his soldiers and forces them to return to the fort for reinforcements. His troops are unable to join the other two regiments en route to do battle with the Indians.

June 25, 1876 General George Custer and his entire regiment is surrounded and destroyed by Sioux and Cheyenne warriors in the Battle of the Little Bighorn, the most decisive Indian victory of the nineteenth century.

October 1876 Colonel Nelson Miles arrives on the Yellowstone River to take charge of the campaign against the Northern Plains Indians.

February 28, 1877 The government confiscates the Black Hills portion of the Fort Laramie Treaty of 1868, which includes more than seven million acres. The Black Hills Act also states that the reservation Sioux would be given all aid necessary for their survival.

May 1877 Sitting Bull, Gall, and about three hundred others in their band flee to Canada.

May 6, 1877 Oglala warrior Crazy Horse surrenders at Fort Robinson in Nebraska.

May 7, 1877 The end of significant military Sioux resistance is achieved when soldiers subdue a small band of Miniconjou.

September 6, 1877 Crazy Horse is bayoneted to death in a scuffle with a guard at Fort Robinson after being arrested for allegedly planning to lead the Sioux in more violence.

July 19, 1881 Sitting Bull and one hundred eighty-six of the Lakota who remain with him in Canada surrender to authorities at Fort Buford.

Late Summer, 1881 Brule warrior Crow Dog kills chief Spotted Tail without provocation. The former believes the latter has been selling off Lakota land to the railroad companies and is angry that the Indian Bureau built a home for Spotted Tail near the Rosebud Agency.

1883 Sitting Bull is finally released from Fort Randall, where he is a prisoner, to the Standing Rock reservation.

1885 Buffalo Bill Cody lures Sitting Bull into his Wild West Show. Sitting Bull proves to be an immensely popular attraction.

1887 The General Allotment Act provides presidential power to reduce the landholdings of Indians across the nation by allotting one hundred sixty acres to the heads of Indian families and eighty acres to individuals. What was left over was to be sold to white settlers.

January 1, 1889 Paiute medicine man Wovoka falls into a trance and claims to have spoken to Jesus and God, who informed him that he would remove the white man from the continent by the spring and resurrect all the dead Indians and dead wildlife, allowing the Native Americans to live in peace and prosperity as hunters again. Wovoka claims that the Indians must perform the Ghost Dance for such an occurrence to become a reality. He sets out to teach it to any Indian willing to listen and learn.

1889 What remains of the Great Sioux Reservation is broken up further by an agreement that divides it by tribe into six separate areas. Land was to be left over for white settlement.

Fall 1889 A Lakota delegation consisting of Kicking Bear, Short Bull, and others travel to Nevada to learn the Ghost Dance from Wovoka. The dance impresses them, and full of hope, they return to teach it to their fellow tribesmen.

Spring 1890 With drought, disease, and desperation plaguing the Lakota tribes on the reservations, they see the Ghost Dance as a path to salvation and practice it continually. The new dance alarms many white citizens and officials who fear it is a prelude to war.

October 1890 Daniel Royer becomes the new Indian agent at Pine Ridge. Fearful and misunderstanding of the Ghost Dance, he requests seven hundred troops to quell what he perceived as an outbreak of Indian militancy.

December 15, 1890 Indian police attempting to arrest Hunkpapa chief Sitting Bull kill him at his home on the Standing Rock reservation. He at first agrees to succumb to the arrest, but is urged by his band to resist, leading to the exchange of gunfire that results in his death. Hundreds of Indians flee to join the Ghost Dancers in the Badlands or Big Foot's band that had left the Cheyenne River Reservation for freedom along the Little Missouri River.

December 28, 1890 Facing arrest, ailing Miniconjou chief Big Foot and his band begin a trek to turn themselves in at the Pine Ridge agency. Major Whitside and his Seventh Cavalry intercept the group and escort them to Wounded Knee Creek. Whitside calls for reinforcements and troops commanded by Colonel James Forsyth arrive that evening. Many soldiers get drunk on whisky and harass the Indians throughout the night.

December 29, 1890 Colonel Forsyth and his Seventh Cavalry men attempt to disarm the Indians at Wounded Knee Creek, resulting in the death of about three hundred Lakota and about thirty soldiers in an orgy of violence. The shooting begins when soldiers try to wrestle a gun away from a deaf Miniconjou and it discharges. Many Indians and some soldiers are killed instantly, after which the troops chase after Indian men, women, and children and shoot them down as far as three miles away.

January 1891 A Court of Inquiry exonerates and reinstates Colonel Forsyth after Colonel Nelson Miles charges him with negligence for his actions at Wounded Knee and strips him of his commission. Meanwhile, the last Lakota resistance ends fairly peacefully after hundreds who were angered by the massacre flee to practice the Ghost Dance and live in freedom in the Badlands. The renegade Indians quickly return to their reservations.

ONE

Setting the Stage

ABOUT THE TIME Christopher Columbus embarked on his epic journey from Spain to the New World, one Indian nation was embarking on a journey of a far less voluntary nature.

Well before the Lakota roamed the northern American Plains, they lived as much as a thousand miles away, possibly in the Ohio Valley or in the Southeast. But they were driven out by the warlike and powerful Iroquois late in the fifteenth century and migrated to the northwest. They eventually settled in what is now northern Minnesota, where they hunted freely in the forest and gathered wild rice growing in marshes.

The Lakota were discovered in the 1600s by Colonial Europeans, who referred to them as the Sioux, which was a name extracted from the Ojibwa word for snake—*nadoweisiw*—translated by white people to mean "enemy."

The Lakota quickly established themselves as a dominant force in the region. They were divided into seven tribes. The Wahpekute, Mdewakanton, Sisseton, and Wahpeton were classified as Santee or "Dakota" Sioux. The Yankton and Yanktonais were "Nakota" and the Teton were "Lakota." The Sioux tribes overwhelmed rivals such as the Cree and Ojibwa until the middle of the seventeenth century. By that time the Europeans were regularly trading Cree and Ojibwa goods such as furs for firearms, which shifted the balance of Indian power in the area. The Sioux simply couldn't survive fighting with bows and arrows against guns.

That forced them to become nomadic once again. One after another, their tribes migrated south and then west into the open territory. There they discovered seemingly endless herds of buffalo roaming the Plains. The buffalo provided everything the Sioux required, including food and hides for clothing and shelter. Around the turn of the eighteenth century, the Lakota joined their fellow tribes in the move westward, which lasted about one hundred years. The Sioux continued to spread out beyond the Missouri River, forcing out Indian tribes such as the Omaha and Iowa along the way. They thrived as hunters of a variety of game, but especially buffalo. As the eighteenth century progressed, they too acquired firearms through fur companies that sponsored annual trade fairs on the Plains.

The buffalo wasn't the only animal to provide the Sioux great benefits. Later in the 1700s their association with the white man brought them into contact with horses, which had become extinct in North America several thousand years ago, but were brought back by the Spanish in the early 1500s. In fact, Ponce de Leon took horses with him in his exploration of Florida. They were also ridden and subsequently bred by conquistadors who invaded what is now the American southwest. Some escaped and others were eventually traded to the Indians. Among the first Indian peoples to use horses were the Pueblo of New Mexico. They had been enslaved by the Spanish, but revolted in the 1680s and drove them out. The fleeing Spanish left their horses, which benefited the Pueblo and other tribes, including the Apache, who became expert riders. Horses were soon swapped and stolen by a number of Indian tribes and eventually arrived in the Northern Plains and into the hands of the Lakota.

Now the Lakota had been thrust into modern times. They had horses and guns, which made them the dominant force in the region. They continued to expand their horizons throughout the Great Plains, east to west from the Missouri River to the Bighorn Mountains and north to south from the Canadian prairies down into what is now Kansas. They also broke into seven tribes with telling and colorful monikers: the Oglala (Scatters Their Own), Miniconjou (Planters by Water), Two Kettle, Sans Arc (Without Bows), Siha Sapa (Blackfeet), Brule, and Hunkpapa. The Brule were particularly adventurous, blazing the trail westward. The Hunkpapa were known as Campers at the Opening of the Circle for their penchant to take the outermost position when camping with other tribes, thereby exposing themselves to the greatest danger in the threat of an attack.

The Seeds of Conflict

A turning point in the relationship between the Sioux and those of European ancestry occurred on September 24, 1804. About 1,000 Brule Lakota under the leadership of Chief Tatanka Sapa (Black Buffalo) were encamped near the mouth of the Bad River, which empties into the Missouri in what is now central South Dakota. They were filled with self-satisfaction and pride after having defeated in battle warriors from the neighboring Omaha, killing seventy-five and capturing forty-eight women and children.

On that fateful day, they heard that a group of white men in boats and pirogues were rowing up the Missouri River. This news didn't startle them. On the contrary, it brought a measure of anticipation to Black Buffalo and his tribe. After all, three teenage Lakota boys had met some male travelers a day earlier and had received from them tobacco and the word that they would like to meet their chiefs the following day. Most often white trappers and fur companies who owned such boats sent men out to trade with them. The Lakota believed the men rowing toward them would no different from the others.

In this case the group of men made up the U.S. Corps of Discovery under the military command of Captain Meriwether Lewis and Lieutenant William Clark. Their travels would later become renowned as the Lewis and Clark Expedition, which eventually made its way to the Great Northwest. They were motivated by the curiosity of the American government, which had recently purchased the entire area from France and sent the men out for a grand exploration. But they were certainly not ordered to make enemies of Native Americans. On the contrary, they were told by President Thomas Jefferson to be quite friendly and draw the Indian population toward friendship with the United States, which, after all, was only twenty-eight years old at the time. When they came into contact with the Indians, they were supposed to simply dicker with them.

But the suspicion on both sides that would grow into a war between the Sioux (and other Indian nations) and representative of the American government, which would last nearly throughout the century, seized the moment on September 27, 1804. Tensions grew when the Brule became dissatisfied with what the U.S. Corps of Discovery was offering in trade. About 200 Lakota wielding guns, spears, and bows and arrows defiantly stood on the shore, preventing the white men from returning to their boats. They held on to the ropes of the boats and demanded tobacco. Lewis and Clark finally agreed and tossed several pounds of tobacco ashore, but by that time their men had been on the verge of lighting a cannon and starting what presumably would have been a bloody battle. The encounter certainly proved to be a precursor of future events.

It also proved, to a certain extent, to be the Lakota's undoing. The Sioux people, as well as Indian nations throughout much of America, eventually grew dependent on goods provided by whites, including pots and pans for cooking, guns, cloth, and various tools. In 1825, the Lakota and other Indian peoples living to the east signed a treaty with the American government, stating that both sides recognized each other's sovereignty. The United States was particularly intimidated by the strength of the Sioux. In fact, the Lakota considered the United States a weaker nation and signed the agreement primarily to establish itself as the dominant force in the region.

Underestimating U.S. Strength

The United States, however, was already stronger than what the Lakota perceived and was growing in strength by the year. The Sioux also didn't realize that the white man would soon weaken their status as the most powerful tribe on the Plains. Whites began infiltrating Lakota territory and settling into the area by the 1830s. Meanwhile, the American government started placing forts in the region to establish itself militarily, thereby posing a great threat to all Indian tribes.

The Brule were by the late 1700s living in what was known as the White River Country of southwestern South Dakota. It was plentiful not only in grass and water but also game such as bison, deer, and an antelope-like mammal called a "pronghorn." It was an ideal situation for mounted hunters such as the Brule, who even benefited from the horses running wild in the southern region of their territory. The Brule assumed control of the area from the Arikara, who were farmers rather than hunters and preferred to remain sedentary.

But when the Brule took over, other Lakota tribes began moving in from areas as distant as Minnesota. The different living philosophies of the various peoples resulted in struggles for all. Some of those who had who migrated into the area began cutting cottonwood groves along streams for firewood and chopping off bark to feed their horses. The sheer number of tribesmen that had streamed into the area resulted in a massive amount of hunting and scarcity of game. The explosion of the fur trade following the War of 1812 motivated the Lakota to focus their efforts on using their prey to provide hides for trade rather than as food. A hunter could be secure in the knowledge that a few buffalo could provide food for his family for quite some time. But the trade market seemed unlimited. In the winter of 1829–30 alone, an estimated 6,000 bison hides were shipped for trade to St. Louis from the Black Hills, which was the heart of Lakota country. That figure was unimpressive compared to the 26,000 bison hides, 25,000 pounds of beaver pelts, 37,500 muskrat skins, 4,000 otter, and 150,000 deer hides traded during that same period. In return, the Lakota received such goods as firearms, ammunition, blankets, cooking equipment, and coffee, which they considered a rare and exotic drink.

The Lakota could not have predicted the sheer number of white Americans who would participate in westward expansion. In 1835, the Brule first set their eyes upon a phenomenon that would become all too familiar to them and other Indian tribes— a caravan of canvas-hooded wagons on wheels. Their initial reaction was positive; they even offered the settlers goods for trade and guided them to places where they could find food and water. But by the 1840s the Indians realized that participation in such migration was not limited to a smattering of white adventure-seekers and those searching for new homes. It was an endless and heavy stream of settlers who stripped the land, cut down trees for firewood, and killed the game on which the Brule and their fellow Sioux tribes were so dependent. Soon bands of Lakota began attacking and robbing wagon trains and white hunters, sometimes even stripping them naked and forcing them to walk back to their modes of transportation without clothing.

The federal government was quick to act. Dispatched was Colonel Stephen W. Kearny, who met with the Brule and various other Lakota at a fur-trading outpost in what is now eastern Wyoming just south of the Platte River. His men intimidated the Indians through a demonstration on horseback of sword-wielding wizardry. In a gesture of goodwill, Kearny presented the Indians with presents and warned them to let the wagon trains freely pass.

But the United States didn't have designs on that territory merely to allow settlers to travel through it. Soon the army had placed what became known as Fort Kearny smack in the middle of the Lakota and Pawnee hunting grounds on the Platte River. The army even bought the trading post where Kearny had confronted the Lakota and renamed it Fort Laramie. Wagon trains streamed into the area in increasing numbers. By May 1949 an estimated 4,400 wagon trains carrying about twenty thousand settlers had wheeled through. Many of the whites carried with them diseases that that soon began to take a toll on the Indian population.

Bad News from the Government

In 1851, Fort Laramie had a visitor. It was superintendent of Indian affairs D.D. Mitchell, who reported back some disquieting news. "(I am) much surprised to witness the sad change with a few years and unlooked-for circumstances had produced," he wrote. "The buffalo, upon which (the Indians) rely for food, clothing, shelter, and traffic, are rapidly diminishing. The hordes of emigrants passing through the country seem to have scattered death and disease in all directions. The tribes have suffered much from the small-pox and cholera, and perhaps still more from venereal diseases."[1]

The same year Mitchell paid a visit to Fort Laramie, the U.S. Congress appropriated one hundred thousand dollars toward the negotiation of another treaty with the Lakota. The promise of gifts motivated many of the estimated ten thousand Indians to attend. The treaty signed on September 17 placed boundaries to territories dominated by the Lakota and other tribes. The Lakota were to control a vast region including what is today North Dakota south of the Hear River, South Dakota west of the Missouri River, northwestern Nebraska, and eastern Wyoming between the North Platte River and the western slope of the Black Hills. In return for assurances that white settlers would pass through peacefully, the Lakota agreed to allow the United States to construct roads and outposts, which included forts, on their land. The treaty also stipulated that the government would pay the Indians the equivalent of fifty thousand dollars annually in various and sundry goods and equipment while providing protection from settlers. The U.S. Senate, however, expressed doubt about the prudence of such an arrangement. It shortened the treaty to cover just ten years and authorized the president the power to renew the terms of the agreement every five years.

If either side believed that they had achieved peace in their time, they were badly mistaken. Any good intentions began to wither and die in August 1854, when a group of thirty-one soldiers commanded by the brazen young lieutenant, John L. Grattan, rode into a Lakota camp and attempted to arrest a Miniconjou named High Forehead who had killed an ox belonging to Mormons that had been passing through as part of a wagon train. Though Grattan's target was a Miniconjou, the vast majority of those residing in the approximately two hundred lodges were Brule. Like many of the army officers fresh out of West Point at the time, Grattan believed he could subdue the entire Lakota nation with a few soldiers and a bit of artillery and he was eager to prove it. Upon his arrival at the camp, Grattan ordered his men into battle formation. Sioux leader Bear That Scatters offered two cows, which was summarily rejected. Grattan then ordered his men to fire into the village, whereupon Bear That Scatters was hit—he later died from his wounds. But the result was more than just a comeuppance for Grattan. He and all his men were killed. It marked the first time U.S. troops were killed in battle against the Lakota.

For a time it seemed the incident would be merely a dot in the landscape of Army-Indian relations. Following the annihilation of Grattan's men, the Lakota picked up where they had left off, raiding Crow and Pawnee villages, hunting buffalo and participating in the Sun Dance, a spiritual undertaking intended to promote unity among all Lakota. But after some began stealing horses and other goods at government-controlled trading posts in 1855, revenge for the killing of Grattan and his men was soon to follow.

Actually, plans for an attack had already started. It was being formulated by Brigadier General William S. Harney from his base at Fort Leavenworth, Kansas. Indian agents warned the Lakota and convinced the vast majority to move their camps from the north to the south side of the Platte River. They were told that any Indians remaining north of the river would be considered hostile and subject to attack.

Most of the Lakota did as they were told, which spoke volumes about their growing fear of the white man. But many of the Brule did not submit so easily. About two hundred fifty remained encamped on a Platte tributary called Bluewater. Among them was a young warrior who had gained increasing respect from his fellow tribesman named Spotted Tail, who had been given that name because he had always attached a raccoon tail to his headdress into battle. By the tender age of sixteen, Spotted Tail had earned a sparkling reputation as a warrior. In those early years, he was fervently militaristic and anti-white.

Upon learning that the group of Brule had remained defiant, the U.S. Army demanded the surrender of Spotted Tail and two other warriors. But the Brule refused to budge. And on the morning of September 3, 1855, Harney and six hundred army soldiers, artillery and all, attacked the Bluewater camp. The Lakota had been accustomed to winning battles, but they were in for a shock. By the time the firing had ceased, eighty-six were dead and seventy women and children had been captured. A wounded Spotted Tail fled while both his wife and child were taken away.

Harney soon added insult to injury. He rode on to Fort Laramie, where he arranged to stop the flow of goods the government had promised even the friendly Lakota. He also stipulated that all trade with the Lakota was to end until Spotted Tail and two other Brule warriors who had killed three whites in a mailwagon attack in 1854 had turned themselves in. Harney then rode off with his troops to attack other villages through the heart of Brule territory. And when the cold weather precluded any more raids, he vowed to return with the spring.

Lakota chiefs who had been unafraid of any force—particularly Americans—a few years earlier, were now frightened. They pleaded with Spotted Tail and the two other warriors to give themselves over to authorities. After all, the loss of three men was inconsequential compared to the loss of trade. The begging paid off. On October 18, 1855, Spotted Tail and the two others, atop their best horses and dressed in full war regalia, rode into Fort Laramie to surrender with the full expectation that they would be put to death for their crime.

They were wrong. Rather than hanging Spotted Tail and the two warriors, the army convinced President Franklin Pierce to pardon them. They allowed the Indians to live in Fort Leavenworth for several months. Spotted Tail softened as he became exposed to American society and fostered friendships with army officers and their families. Many would argue that while he started a new life at Fort Leavenworth, something within Spotted Tail died that winter. He lost his passion for the Sioux way of life and his warrior spirit. But there was a calculated logic to his new attitude. He realized that his Brule could never survive if they sought a fight to the finish against the sheer number of white settlers and the power of the U.S. Army. After all, Fort Leavenworth alone housed more soldiers than the entire Brule nation had warriors. Moreover, it seemed the endless stream of whites infiltrating their territory could no longer be stopped. They were not only passing through in wagon trains, but they were building homes and even towns. And they were changing the lifestyles of other tribes, such as the Delaware, Kaw, and Shawnee, many of whom now wore European-style clothes, farmed the land, and lived in houses. Spotted Tail saw in them the wave of the future for the American Indian.

A Santee Slaughter

The Santee Sioux did not. Hundreds of miles north in Minnesota the Santee watched with disenchantment in the 1850s as 150,000 whites settled upon their lands. Making matters worse, money and food supplies promised them by the U.S. government weren't arriving, causing starvation and anger among the Santee people. And it had become apparent that all efforts by that same government were being made to eliminate the Sioux way of life. Sioux Indian agent Major Thomas Galbraith later confirmed those intentions, explaining:

> "The theory, in substance, was to break up the communal system among the Sioux; weaken and destroy their tribal religion; individualize them by giving each a separate home, and having them subsist by industry—the sweat of their brows; till the soil; make labor honorable and idleness dishonorable; or, as it was expressed in short, 'make white men out of them.'"[2]

Santee chief Big Eagle expressed that his people understood what the white man was attempting to accomplish. But they certainly didn't agree with it.

> "The whites were always trying to make the Indians give up their life and live like white men—go to farming, work hard and do as they did—and the Indians did not know how to do that, and did not want to anyway," he said. "If the Indians had tried to make the whites live like them, the whites would have resisted, and it was the same way with many Indians. . . . Many of the white men often abused the Indians and treated them unkindly. Perhaps they had excuse, but the Indians did not think so. Many of the whites always seemed to say by their manner when they saw an Indian, 'I am better than you,' and the Indians did not like this. . . . The Dakota (Sioux) did not believe there were better men in the world than they."[3]

By 1862, the Santee territory had been reduced to a comparative sliver; about ten miles wide and one hundred fifty miles long. About 6,600 Santee lived there, but other Sioux tribes, including the Mdewakanton, Sisseton, and Yanktonai, also inhabited the area.

Santee Chief Little Crow complained to Galbraith that money had been allocated to take care of his people and the shelves of the distribution stores were well stocked with food. Why, he asked, were they not being fed? Galbraith, who was under orders from the U.S. government to undermine the Santee way of life, turned to Andrew Myrick, who was in charge of the food supplies. Myrick, who ironically had an Indian wife, replied scornfully, "Let them eat grass."[4]

Added to the rising tensions and anger felt by the Santee Sioux, the comment pushed many over the edge. About one hundred young warriors expressed to Little Crow that it was time to wage war on white America. Little Crow answered that it was futile to do so, claiming that no matter how many whites were killed they would simply keep coming. Fellow Santee tribesman Red Middle Voice called Little Crow a coward. Angered, Little Crow again expressed his belief that it was suicide to fight the white man. But he added that he was not a coward and he would prove it by sacrificing his life. The Santee would indeed fight back and Little Crow would lead the way. They embarked on a rampage in late August 1862 that left more than a thousand whites dead. Among the first to be killed was Myrick, who was discovered with a mouthful of grass.

Retribution came harshly and swiftly. Soldiers were dispatched to Fort Ridgely, forcing the Santees to withdraw with two hundred prisoners, including many white women and children and a significant number of bi-racial Indians known to be sympathetic to whites. Little Crow, who couldn't control bands of Santee marauders that were killing defenseless settlers, attempted to concentrate their fury on the soldiers. The Indians held their own against the soldiers until September 22. That day Little Crow sent his finest warriors out to ambush a U.S. army regiment led by Colonel Henry H. Sibley, which was reportedly on the way. But the Indians were routed; many were killed (including a highly respected war chief named Mankato) and were forced to retreat.

That evening the Santee decided that Sibley's soldiers were simply too strong. They debated whether to surrender or make the long trek into the Plains to join their Lakota Sioux cousins.

Little Crow spoke of his shame that seven hundred of his best warriors were defeated soundly by whites, which he described as cowardly women, even though his men were outnumbered by the soldiers, who also had superior weaponry. He ordered that all the tipis be dismantled and that the long trek westward begin. Soon, however, Sibley and his men marched into the Santee camp and demanded the return of the prisoners. He also demanded that all the Santee become prisoners of war until trials could determine the guilty ones, who would then be hanged. Sibley also sent out bi-racial messengers to find more Santee with the word that anyone who didn't surrender voluntarily would be tracked down and captured or killed.

Sibley was good to his word. Since he believed that Indians had no legal rights, no defense counsel was appointed for them. The trials continued into early November, when it was announced that three hundred three Santee had been given death sentences and sixteen others would be imprisoned. But President Abraham Lincoln showed compassion. He refused to authorize their hanging until he reviewed the trial records. The result was that soldiers were forced to protect the condemned Indians from angry white mobs, some of whom intended to lynch the Indians. Sibley kept the other seventeen hundred Santee as prisoners despite the fact they were charged with nothing. White mobs assaulted them. One Indian baby was snatched from his mother's arms and beaten to death. Lincoln informed Sibley that he had found just cause to hang only thirty-nine of the three hundred three men. Thirty-eight were hung in the largest public execution in American history (one had been given a reprieve). The others were sent to prison.

All treaties with the Santee were soon deemed null and void. White citizens of Minnesota were given the opportunity to seize their land without payment. All Indians were to be banished to Dakota country or killed. On May 4, 1863, the first shipment of Santee left St. Paul via steamboat. The river landing was lined by white people taunting and throwing stones at them. The Santee were forced into a reservation at Crow Creek on the Missouri River, where the conditions were far from ideal. Of the thirteen hundred dispatched there, fewer than one thousand survived the first winter.

The Santee had at least one notable visitor that year. A young Teton Sioux witnessed the degradation heaped upon his Indian cousins, who told him stories about how the Americans had driven them from their land. He feared that soon those same Americans would also move in to buffalo country, where his people still flourished. He knew his Sioux tribe must find the courage and means to stop them. That young man was named Tatanka Yotanka: Sitting Bull. He would play a huge role in shaping future events.

John Chivington and the Sand Creek Massacre

Meanwhile, white movement westward through Sioux and Cheyenne hunting grounds intensified in 1858 when gold was discovered around the Platte River in Colorado. Prospectors poured through the region that had been promised various Indian tribes as exclusively theirs by the Fort Laramie Treaty of 1851, which was now in tatters. Miners built homes and villages that laid the foundation for the city of Denver. During negotiations for a new treaty, Cheyenne chiefs Black Kettle and White Antelope and their bands were encamped near Sand Creek. Despite their peaceful actions, rumors ran rampant that an Indian uprising was imminent. Fanning the flames was Reverend John Chivington, who was running for Congress. Among his campaign promises was keeping the citizens of Colorado safe from Indian attack. But Chivington had far more violent and sinister intentions. Told by officers at nearby Fort Lyon that the Cheyenne and Arapaho camping at Sand Creek were peaceful, he replied that he was there to kill Indians.

Chivington was true to his word. Deploying 700 volunteer troops, many of whom were drunk, as well as four howitzers, he led a massacre of the men, women, and children at Sand Creek on November 29, 1864. A white flag had been hoisted, but that didn't stop Chivington, who bragged that 500 Indians were killed, though the number was later lowered to about 30 men and 125 women and children. White Antelope was among those shot down. One witness described the bloody event.

> "They were scalped, their brains knocked out; the men used their knives . . . (and) knocked them in the head with their guns, beat their brains out, mutilated their bodies in every sense of the word."[5]

Though Black Kettle survived, he was murdered four years later by troops led by George Custer in a similar incident.

Meanwhile, Coloradans initially applauded Chivington in the belief that the extermination of Indians, whether peaceful or not, was prudent policy. Chivington became a hero in Denver City, where he regaled audiences with stories about the incident and displayed one hundred scalps, including pubic hair of Indian women, to delighted onlookers. But a congressional investigation in which details of the massacre were revealed forced Chivington to resign and made him a reviled figure.

The Cheyenne vowed never to seek peace again with the white man. Word of the Sand Creek Massacre spread, motivating Cheyenne, Sioux, and Arapaho to launch a series of raids against wagon trains, stage stations, and small military outposts. They torched the town of Julesburg and scalped the defenders to avenge the massacre at Sand Creek. But when they returned to camp to celebrate, they understood well that white soldiers would surely be hunting them down. Most decided they would travel north across the Platte River and join their Northern Cheyenne relatives while Black Kettle and others moved south of the Arkansas River to befriend the Southern Arapaho, Kiowas, and Comanches.

The Cheyenne all camped together on the Powder River until the spring of 1865, when they moved near the Oglala Sioux of Chief Red Cloud. The southern Cheyenne had never seen so many Indians camped together; more than eight thousand Sioux inhabited that spot. Soon they all grew confident that they could ward off any white invaders. Red Cloud would speak about how the white man had taken all the land except that on which his tribe still roamed free and that the "Great Spirit" meant for them to keep it. They set out to prove it in late July when they killed a group of soldiers outside a fort called Platte Bridge Station. They believed that taught the white man the lesson that the Laramie Treaty of 1851 should be respected.

By late August 1865, Cheyenne, Sioux, and Arapaho Indians were scattered throughout Powder River country, from the Bighorn Mountains on the west to the Black Hills on the east. They had grown so certain of their invincibility that they felt skepticism when reports began circulating that soldiers were on their way. But it was true—and one of three troop columns was commanded by General Patrick E. Connor, who had been in charge of the butchering of 278 Paiutes on Bear River two years earlier and had claimed that the Indians north of the Platte River had to be hunted like wolves. A group of Cheyenne and Sioux soon learned that Connor was planning on building a fort in the midst of their hunting grounds, which clued them in on the impending attack.

They tried to warn the Arapaho, but it was too late. Connor's column, with the help of some Pawnee, who had been tribal enemies of the Arapaho, swooped into an Arapaho village and killed more than fifty men, women, and children in what became known as the Battle of Tongue River. The soldiers burned down the village and the Pawnee stole nine hundred horses, which represented about one-third of the Arapaho's total herd. The fleeing Arapaho later found the nine hundred horses dead on the ground. The Pawnee had shot them all in the head.

A group of Cheyenne led by Roman Nose confronted the other two columns of soldiers, who had become exhausted and hungry chasing Indians all over the Plains. Some of the troops were killed and others driven back to the fort. Connor and his men had killed some Arapaho, but certainly didn't accomplish what they had set out to do. The Cheyenne and Sioux remained settled with plenty of buffalo and antelope to hunt over the winter. The hunt for Indians had cost the government thirty million dollars and relatively few warriors had been killed.

But the white men kept coming. In 1864, gold had been discovered in Montana, which prompted the creation of the Bozeman Trail and further violations of Sioux territory guaranteed by the Fort Laramie Treaty. The end of the Civil War brought a flood of whites through the area into Wyoming and finally Montana. Red Cloud and other Sioux chiefs were invited to Fort Laramie to discuss another peace treaty. Though the government had already committed to maintaining the Bozeman Trail and had ordered 700 troops into the area to man a chain of forts in Wyoming and Montana, it was looking to ensure safe passage through negotiations with the Indians. Oglala Sioux chief Red Cloud saw through the deception. He stormed out of the treaty conference upon learning of the forts, asking government leaders why they were negotiating for peace when they had already decided to take the land by force. The peace talks failed.

The Bozeman Trail proved quite unsafe for travelers as Red Cloud's warriors harassed wagon trains, miners, soldiers, and men building the forts. Undaunted, the U.S. government remained steadfast in its plans to build the forts, among them Fort Phil Kearny on the slopes of the Bighorn Mountains, the finest hunting ground of the Plains Indians. In late December 1866, Fort Kearny commander Captain William Fetterman, who had bragged he could destroy the entire Sioux nation with eighty men, led a group of soldiers into northern Wyoming to track down several Lakota warriors who had attacked a detail of men chopping wood near the fort. To prove his point, Fetterman left the fort with exactly eighty men. Among the warriors they pursued was a young man named Crazy Horse, who was gaining great respect among his fellow Sioux and would eventually become a legend.

Fetterman, however, was careless. The taunting Lakota drew him into an ambush. Several hundred Sioux and Cheyenne warriors awaited him and his eighty men. Fetterman met his doom at the hands of an Oglala Sioux named American Horse, who slit his throat. The Fetterman Massacre resulted in the killing of all of the soldiers.

But during the Indian Wars of the nineteenth century, nary an Indian triumph was met without cries for revenge. The cries in this case came from General William Tecumseh Sherman, fresh off the bloodbath he was greatly responsible for during his march from Atlanta in the Civil War. Sherman told General Philip Sheridan to command his troops in a war that would lead to the "extermination—the utter annihilation of these Indians." Sherman added that the Indian was an enemy of white civilization and that, in regard specifically to the Lakota, even women and children needed to die.

The government had other ideas. They sent Sherman to the Union Pacific Railroad track in western Nebraska to try to convince the Indians to sign a treaty that would allow trains to chug through their territory peacefully. But when Sherman spoke, he dropped a bombshell. He proposed that the Indians move up the Missouri River and away from the sacred hunting grounds they had embraced for generations. The wild game that was the life-blood of the Sioux did not exist where Sherman was proposing they relocate. The offer was refused.

Undaunted, the government set up another peace council in the spring of 1868. This time Sherman was under strict orders to offer the elimination of the forts on the Powder River road and convince Red Cloud to sign a treaty. Sherman and his peace commission sent agents to invite Red Cloud to Fort Laramie, but the Oglala chief said he would only talk if the forts were first abandoned. Red Cloud and his allies kept a close watch on the forts. On July 29 the troops at Fort C.F. Smith left. Red Cloud and his warriors celebrated by burning down the post. A month later, a group of Cheyenne torched Fort Phil Kearny after it too was abandoned. Soon all the forts that dotted the Powder River road had been closed. Red Cloud had won his war.

The second Fort Laramie Treaty gave what is now the western half of South Dakota, including the Black Hills, to the Sioux. But the Lakota also ceded their hunting grounds in what is now North Dakota, eastern Wyoming, and northern Nebraska. But what the Indians didn't understand was that it also stipulated that they must remain on reservations, straying only to hunt. They were also to stay away from military posts and railroad construction. That was a key point to the government, which planned on soon completing the ambitious transcontinental project. The Sioux couldn't fathom the enormity of that development. Wagon trains had merely passed through their territory. The railroad would create new towns on Lakota lands and allow sport and commercial hunters to wipe out game on Sioux hunting grounds.

Whites never did move out of Lakota territory completely. Several forts remained and General Philip Sheridan even invited the sportsmen of the United States and Great Britain to the American West to hunt buffalo. Thousands accepted the invitation; it was not unusual to see rifles pointed out of both sides of a train, which would slow down to allow them to shoot accurately. The number of buffalo, on which the Lakota and other tribes had become so dependent for food, clothing, and other necessities, was dwindling rapidly and alarmingly. Hunters were not only killing buffalo for sport. Buffalo hides had grown in value back east for items such as furniture upholstery, shoes, and saddles. A talented marksman could kill fifty buffalo a day or more. Only the hides were taken, leaving the rest of the buffalo to rot. Dead carcasses were strewn about the region. It has been estimated that over four million buffalo were killed during a two-year period in the early 1870s.

Another development weakened Sioux resolve and heightened their frustration. During a trip taken by several Indian chiefs to Washington, D.C., in acceptance of an invitation by President Ulysses S. Grant, Red Cloud and others saw the enormity of white civilization and came away convinced that the Indian people would be overwhelmed militarily and in sheer numbers if they attempted to resist.

Notes

1. Di Silvestro, Roger L. *In The Shadow of Wounded Knee*. New York: Walker and Company, 2005. 27.

2. Clodfelter, Michael. *The Dakota War: The United States Army versus the Sioux, 1862–1865*. Jefferson, N.C.: McFarland and Company, 1998. 38.

3. Brown, Dee. *Bury My Heart at Wounded Knee*. New York: Henry Holt and Company, 1970. 38.

4. Lewis, John E. *The Mammoth Book of Native Americans*. New York: Carroll & Graf Publishers, 2004. 172.

5. Viola, Herman J. *Little Bighorn Remembered: The Untold Story of Custer's Last Stand*. New York: Times Books, 1999. 5.

6. Di Silvestro, Roger L. *In the Shadow of Wounded Knee*. New York: Walker and Company, 2005. 33–34.

TWO

Bighorn and Beyond

THE EXCURSION TAKEN BY Red Cloud and other chiefs to visit Washington, D.C., was the brainchild of Ely Parker, a one-time Seneca Indian chief who was now representing the Board of Indian Commissioners in the nation's capital. Parker became alarmed at the increasing violence on the Plains and became quite concerned by the spring of 1870 about the threat of a full-scale war between the Indians and the United States. He was also cognizant of the insistence of Oglala chief Red Cloud to keep the territory ensured by the Treaty of 1868 and of the rebelliousness of Spotted Tail and his Brule despite the fact that they had agreed to live on the Fort Randall reservation along the Missouri River.

Parker sent a direct invitation to Spotted Tail to visit President Grant. He also dispatched a messenger to invite Red Cloud to the White House as well. Both were intrigued by the offer. Red Cloud yearned to speak to the Great Father about Sioux concerns, including their distaste for the notion of living on a reservation. Parker was thrilled to learn that both had accepted. He sent Colonel John E. Smith out to escort Red Cloud, who chose fifteen fellow Oglala to travel with him on the Union Pacific Railroad. The ride on what was termed by many at the time as the "Iron Horse" was fascinating and frightening at the same time. Stops in Omaha and particularly Chicago opened Indian eyes to the sheer mass of white humanity in the country, as well as to the advanced technology that created towering buildings that appeared to almost reach the clouds.

Five days after setting off on the journey, the Indians reached the capital, where they had reservations set for them at the

Washington House Hotel on Pennsylvania Avenue. Red Cloud was astounded to see Spotted Tail and a group of Brule there. Parker worried that the two chiefs would clash since the latter had obeyed the government by agreeing to move his people to Fort Randall and the former believed Indians had no business on a reservation. But Spotted Tail greeted Red Cloud warmly and proceeded to complain that he and his tribe abhorred life on the reservation and wished to return to the hallowed hunting grounds in Nebraska.

The next day, Parker played the role of tour guide, showing the Sioux around Washington, which included a visit to the Senate in session. The Indians were given white man's clothing to wear, which made them uncomfortable both physically and emotionally. In fact, Red Cloud expressed as much to Parker, who provided him with buckskins, blankets, and moccasins to wear during dinner with President Grant. That affair featured not only the leader of the United States but also cabinet members, foreign diplomats, and congressmen who gawked at the sight of Indians in the midst of a fancy official event. Spotted Tail enjoyed the taste of strawberries, prompting him to exclaim that the white man obviously had superior culinary delights than what was being sent to his tribe at Fort Randall.

Then they got down to the business of attempting to establish a lasting peace. Secretary of the Interior Jacob Cox offered the Indians guns and ammunition for hunting, but only if peace was ensured. Red Cloud interpreted that to mean a move to a reservation, which he promptly rejected. He spoke of his skepticism of the U.S. government and of his purpose of coming to Washington, which was to express displeasure. He explained to Cox that Spotted Tail and his Brule lived on a reservation and were miserable. He called representatives of the United States who have negotiated treaties with the Indians liars. He asked Cox to tell President Grant just that. And he told Parker all he wanted was for his people to be free to live in the wild and kill game, though he admitted that the day would come when he would be forced to live like a white man as well.

Soon the Indians were meeting with President Grant in the executive office of the White House, where Red Cloud repeated the same concerns and stressing that the Oglala did not wish to live on the Missouri River. He added that the Treaty of 1868 was designed to bring assurances that his people had the right to trade at Fort Laramie and have an agency available on the Platte. Grant didn't address those issues specifically, but he replied that he would make certain that justice would be served. What Grant did know and didn't tell Red Cloud was that the language in the Treaty of 1868 that the Congress ratified made no mention of Fort Laramie or an agency on the Platte. The wording had been changed, unbeknownst to the Indians.

Grant told Cox and Parker in private to explain the revised terms of the document to the Sioux. The latter knew the Indians would feel they'd been cheated. After Cox went over it in detail the next morning, Red Cloud exclaimed that this was the first time he'd heard of such a treaty, claiming it was nothing like the one he'd signed. Cox countered that he didn't believe the commissioners at Fort Laramie would have lied to the Indians about the contents of the document. Red Cloud answered that he didn't feel the commissioners falsified the facts, either, but that it was misinterpreted. Cox offered to meet with Red Cloud again and gave him a copy of the treaty to take with him, but the Oglala chief declined, complaining that the treaty was full of lies.

The Sioux discussed returning home the next day, but how could they explain to their people that the Treaty of 1868 was not what they had believed it to be? Parker convinced them to meet one more time with Cox, who greeted them by saying he was sorry the Sioux had misunderstood the wording of the treaty. The conciliatory Secretary of the Interior added that although the Powder River country was outside the area in which they were permitted to live, it was inside their agreed-upon hunting grounds and that they were welcome to live there. Cox also said they could trade their goods outside the reservation.

Red Cloud was placated. He told Parker he was ready to board the train for home, but was then told of a surprise trip to New York City that the government had planned for him and his people. Red Cloud replied that he preferred to head home because he had seen enough white people, but was convinced to go when Parker told him he had been invited to make a speech to the people of New York. And when he arrived, he was stunned at the rousing ovation he received from the white audience. He asked them to help keep the peace and complained to them that the Sioux had been deceived by the whites who had served as inter-preters of the treaty, which the Indians could not read.

Gold in the Black Hills

The event that most angered the tribes was the finding of gold in the Black Hills in 1874. Following that discovery, their world would never be the same. The U.S. Cavalry sent ten companies under the command of Colonel George Custer to the Black Hills to investi-gate the claim that gold had been found. The excursion drew the ire of the many Indian tribes that inhabited the region. Their voices were loud enough to be heard by President Grant, who stated that he was determined to keep intruders out of the Black Hills, which, after all, had been guaranteed the Indians in the Treaty of 1868. But after a two-month mission, Custer returned with the claim that gold was everywhere and prospectors streamed into th2e area.

The U.S. Army made a feeble attempt to close the Black Hills, but by the following year thousands of prospectors were digging away and panning for gold in the mountains deemed sacred by the Sioux nation. So the government simply offered to purchase the Black Hills. They figured that most of the Lakota were living on agencies that provided all their resources for them and that they certainly had no use for gold, so they did not need the Black Hills. But two Lakota in particular disagreed. They were Sitting Bull and Crazy Horse, whose people continued to live the nomadic lives of hunters despite the shrinking number of wild game and seemingly unending white encroachment. And they had vowed not to give up the Black Hills without a fight. The government offer of six millions dollars to buy the Black Hills was refused.

Grant had another idea. He issued an edict directed at all nomadic tribes in the West, but particularly the Lakota, that all of them had to report to a reservation by January 31, 1876, or risk being labeled as hostile and subject to arrest. Grant

believed once all Sioux lived on reservations they would be subdued and far more willing to sell the Black Hills at what was
perceived as a reasonable price.

Early that same year, Sitting Bull had asked all Lakota to
gather for discussions about the continuing infiltration of white
people on their land, though it is not known whether he was
aware of Grant's ultimatum at that time. What Sitting Bull certainly didn't know was that the U.S. Army was planning a
three-way pincer movement against the Lakota that summer
around the Powder River-Yellowstone region intended to trap
the Indians. Coincidentally, the meeting Sitting Bull suggested
was to be held at Chalk Buttes, which is precisely where the
army planned on trapping them.

Free-roaming Indians poured in from throughout the region,
not just to meet with Sitting Bull, but in a show of unity and
strength. Sioux tribesmen organized in a huge encampment at
the Little Bighorn River in Montana. Some Sioux left their reservations to join in. Seven thousand other Sioux, Cheyenne, and
Arapaho had also migrated to a three-mile stretch along the
river.

Early in June, Sitting Bull had fifty pieces of flesh cut off his
body in preparation for the annual sun dance. He stared at the
sun until he fell into a trance. He believed he had received a
vision of soldiers falling from the sky like grasshoppers right
into the Indian camp. They had no ears because they had
refused to listen. Sitting Bull told his fellow tribesmen that the
Great Spirit had provided those "Bluecoats" to be killed.

That was all Crazy Horse needed to hear. He had waited for
years for the opportunity to test himself as a warrior against
U.S. soldiers. He had even studied how the army fought and
designed strategies he believed were the best ways to defeat
them. He often dreamed of the day he could be given the opportunity to lead his Oglala Sioux warriors to victory. And that day
came on June 17, 1876, after a hunting party had seen a column
of Bluecoats under the command of General George Crook and it
was decided that about five hundred Sioux and Northern Cheyenne warriors, including Crazy Horse and Sitting Bull, would
ride through the night to confront them. Those soldiers belonged

to the Seventh Cavalry. The Battle of the Little Bighorn was about to begin.

Crazy Horse had determined that striking weak links on the enemy line and moving swiftly from one spot to another would confuse and frustrate the soldiers commanded by Crook. And that's what they did after they had ridden fifty miles into Crook's camp. The result was a victory for the warriors in which they consistently kept the soldiers on the defensive. Crook, in fact, was forced to return to his base camp for reinforcements.

The Battle of the Little Bighorn

Following that skirmish, the chiefs decided to move their camp to the valley of the Greasy Grass, otherwise known as Little Bighorn. By that time at least ten-thousand Indians, including about four-thousand Sioux and Cheyenne warriors, were encamped in the area. They were not only content in the knowledge that they had whipped a column of soldiers, but by the fact that in those days of dwindling game populations, antelope and even buffalo were found nearby. Though a number of chiefs were present and all tribes considered themselves as equals, one stood above the rest. And that was Sitting Bull.

The Indians had not seen any Bluecoats since the battle against Crook, which Sitting Bull didn't believe qualified as the fulfillment of his vision of soldiers falling into the Indian camp. But on June 24, scouts reported that soldiers were marching toward Little Bighorn. They were right—Custer and his men were on the way and they were in a hurry. The Sioux mounted their horses, grabbed their guns, and rode off to fight. The women and children mounted their horses and galloped off in the opposite direction.

The warriors didn't realize that a column of soldiers commanded by Major Marcus Reno was attacking a Blackfoot Sioux camp until they heard gunfire rattling from that direction. Reno's men had come in firing. Sioux warriors raced into the area on horseback. Then came the Cheyenne.

"I rode swiftly toward Sitting Bull's camp," said *Cheyenne* chief Two Moon. "Then I saw the white soldiers (Reno's men) fighting in a line.

Indians covered the flat. They began to drive the soldiers all mixed up—Sioux, then soldiers, then more Sioux, and all shooting. The air was full of smoke and dust. I saw the soldiers fall back and drop into the riverbed like buffalo fleeing."[1]

The Sioux hero in that attack was a muscular war chief named Gall, who had been adopted as Sitting Bull's younger brother and had distinguished himself as both a hunter and warrior. Reno's initial attack all but destroyed Gall's family, but he still had the presence of mind to direct his tribesmen in battle. He also understood that the retreat of that column allowed him to divert hundreds of warriors for a frontal attack against Custer's men while Crazy Horse and Two Moon attacked the flank and rear. Hundreds of Sioux and Cheyenne had surrounded the man they called "Long Hair." The result was a massacre.

"We circled all around (Custer)—swirling like water round a stone," Two Moon explained. "We shoot, we ride fast, we shoot again. Soldiers drop, and horses fall on them. . . . Indians keep swirling round and round, and the soldiers killed only a few. Many soldiers fell. . . . Once in a while some man would break out and run towards the river, but he would fall.

"At last about 100 men and five horse men stood on the hill all bunched together. All along the bugler kept blowing his commands. . . . Then a chief was killed. I hear it was (Custer). I don't know. . . . One man all alone ran far down toward the river, then round up over the hill. I thought he was going to escape, but a Sioux fired and hit him in the head. He was the last man."[2]

The Indian warriors killed 260 soldiers, including 212 of Custer's men. Only 30 tribesmen lost their lives. Toward the end of the battle, some soldiers raised their arms and asked for mercy, but the Indians showed no pity, killing them all. Miniconjou warrior White Bull took pride in his belief that he personally had killed Custer, though other tribesmen who laid claim to that distinction were Rain-in-the-Face, Flat Hip, and Brave Bear.

Many of Reno's soldiers still lived. They were entrenched on a hill down the river along with reinforcements commanded by Major Frederick Benteen. The Indians surrounded the hill and maintained a close eye, and then began battling the soldiers the following morning. But that day, scouts sent out by the chiefs reported back that they had seen more soldiers who appeared to be heading in the direction of the Little Bighorn. Those soldiers, who were led by Generals Alfred Terry and John Gibbon, noticed figures lying on the ground from miles away. They believed them at first to be dead buffalo carcasses rotting after a hunt. But when they got closer, they realized to their horror that they were hundreds of dead soldiers and horses.

The Sioux and Cheyenne could not celebrate their victory. They knew from experience that their triumphs only motivated the white man to seek revenge. And since what became immortalized as the Battle of the Little Bighorn was the most decisive and bloody Indian triumph, they realized that soldiers would soon be tracking them down. They had won the battle, but they knew they couldn't win the war. They understood that the sheer numerical superiority of the white race precluded any opportunity to win a prolonged conflict. They also knew from past experience that any Indian triumph would result in a call for swift and merciless revenge.

The warriors had used up most of their ammunition, which precluded any thought of fighting yet more troops. They understood the foolishness of trying to battle well-armed U.S. military units with bows and arrows. So they decided to break camp. The various tribes separated and traveled in different directions. But when word of the destruction of the Seventh Cavalry reached white America, it was deemed a slaughter perpetrated by red savages and the cries for revenge were numerous, swift, and fierce.

A New Government Edict

The first reaction of the government was to enact a new law to assume military control of all reservations in the Sioux country. On August 15, 1876, it was declared that all Indians living in the Powder River territory and Black Hills, most of whom were on reservations and had nothing to do with the Battle of the Little Bighorn, must give up all rights to that land. The explanation was that the Indians had violated the Treaty of 1868 by going to war against the United States, though just a comparatively small group of Sioux and Cheyenne had done that and only when first attacked by Reno's men.

A new commission was dispatched to the reservations in September to convince the chiefs on the reservations to sign legal documents transferring the Black Hills to the United States. Among those who spoke at the Red Cloud agency was Bishop Henry Whipple, who first explained that the Black Hills and Powder River country must be vacated, rations would hence-forth be received on the Missouri River, and the United States would be permitted to build three roads through what had been their reservation leading into the Black Hills. Whipple then did his best to weaken the resolve of Red Cloud and his fellow tribesmen.

> "The Great Father said that his heart was full of tenderness for his red children," he said, "and he selected this commission of friends of the Indians that they might devise a plan, as he directed them, in order that the Indian nations might be saved, and that instead of growing smaller and smaller until the last Indian looks upon his own grave, they might become as the white has become, a great and powerful people."[3]

Whipple had expressed the perception of many whites that Indians should strive to own property and farm the land. In fact, the Treaty of 1868 had included several incentives for Indians to do just that. But the Sioux that gathered to hear Whipple and the other representatives of the government that day couldn't understand how they were to be saved as a nation by agreeing to move to the Missouri River and away from their hunting grounds and the Black Hills, which had been ceded to them many years earlier. And they were not afraid to speak their minds on that subject. Spotted Tail as well as fellow chiefs No Heart and Red Dog spoke bitterly about broken promises and betrayal. So did Brule chief Standing Elk.

> "My friend, your words are like a man knocking me in the head with a club," he said. "By your speech you have put great fear upon us. What-ever you white people ask of us, wherever we go, we always say 'yes,

yes, yes!' Whenever we don't agree to what is asked of us in council, you always reply, 'You won't get anything to eat! You won't get anything to eat!' "[4]

Spotted Tail stated he would not sign the treaty unless he was invited to Washington to speak with President Grant. The commissioners presented the chiefs with a one-week deadline to sign, but it soon became obvious they would not lay their hands upon the pen.

It didn't matter. The commissioners indicated they would cut off all rations, remove them all to the Indian Territory in the south, and confiscate all their guns and horses. The Indians had no choice. Soon Red Cloud, Spotted Tail, and the others were signing away the Black Hills. The commissioners then visited agencies at Standing Rock, Cheyenne River, Crow Creek, Lower Brule, and Santee and intimidated the chiefs of other Sioux tribes to sign the treaty. The Black Hills, which the Sioux believed the Great Spirit had given to them, had been taken away. Miners poured into the area looking for gold and the wild game on which the Sioux had survived was soon gone.

The United States wasn't done avenging the Battle of the Little Bighorn. Four weeks after Red Cloud and Spotted Tail signed the treaty, eight companies of the cavalry marched into agency camps, arrested all male Indians and rounded up all the ponies and guns. The horses were to remain so they could transport all the goods used by the reservation Indians to Fort Robinson, where all the tribesmen were being relocated so they could be under the watchful eyes of the soldiers.

The army then went searching both north and west of the Black Hills for stray Sioux, killing those they could find. A detachment commanded by Colonel Anson Mills attacked a village of Oglalas and Miniconjous led by chief American Horse, which had recently departed from Crazy Horse's camp on Grand River and were headed south for the winter to their reservation. The Sioux fought back and many escaped, but four warriors and fifteen women and children were trapped in a cave at the end of a canyon. When cavalry reinforcements arrived, soldiers fired into the cave, but American Horse and his warriors shot back, killing two soldiers and wounding nine. A scout was sent into the cave to speak to the Sioux, informing them that they would be left unharmed if they surrendered. American Horse managed to crawl out, but he had been struck in the groin by a bullet and was soon dead.

Meanwhile, the Sioux that had escaped spread the word of the attack on the American Horse village to the camp of Sitting Bull and Gall. About six hundred warriors arrived to help, but it was too late. The Indians didn't have enough ammunition to mount an effective attack. All they could do was rescue the survivors and bury the dead. Sitting Bull understood that he must take his tribe far from the soldiers, so they traveled north along the Yellowstone, where some of the few buffalo left on the continent remained. Gall and his hunting party stumbled upon a wagon train of soldiers taking supplies to yet another new fort, which was being built along the Yellowstone River. When he learned of the construction, Sitting Bull sent a friendly note to the commander of the soldiers asking them to leave Sioux territory. Lieutenant Colonel Elwell Otis returned the message with one of his own: If the Sioux wanted a fight, his soldiers could provide one.

Sitting Bull still yearned for peace. He sent a messenger bearing a white flag to the wagon train, which was now led by Colonel Nelson Miles, who was flanked by more soldiers. Miles agreed to meet with Sitting Bull. He accused the Hunkpapa chief of hating the white man and asked him what he was doing in Yellowstone country. Sitting Bull answered that he was there to hunt buffalo and feed and clothe his people. Miles informed him that there was a reservation for Sitting Bull and his tribesmen, but that news was met with indignation. Sitting Bull was not about to agree to live on a reservation. He planned instead to spend the winter where he believed the Sioux belonged—in the Black Hills.

Miles and Sitting Bull met again the next day, but their discussion disintegrated into a series of accusations. The Sioux chief offered that the Great Spirit had made him a free Indian, not one who could be tied to an agency, dependent on the white man to survive. And when the meeting was over, Sitting Bull told his warriors that they needed to scatter because he was certain that soldiers were going to attack again.

He was right. On November 25, troops commanded by Colonel Ranald Mackenzie discovered the Cheyenne camp of chief Dull Knife in Wyoming, which had gained statehood seven years earlier. The village was destroyed, but many of the Cheyenne escaped north and joined Crazy Horse and his Sioux on the Tongue River. Little more than a month later, Miles attacked that camp. The soldiers and Sioux fought several battles in the bitter cold, which resulted in the loss of supplies for the Indians, who again scattered in different directions. Crazy Horse grew desperate. He was accompanied by fewer than one hundred thirty warriors and little ammunition and he was insecure in the knowledge that the warmth of spring would allow the soldiers to return and destroy whatever new village his tribe created.

Sitting Bull Heads North

By that time, Sitting Bull had made a fateful decision. He and his Hunkpapa would flee to Canada in the belief that there was no room in the United States for the white man and his people. He had first searched for Crazy Horse to try to convince him to accompany him to the nation up north, but the Oglala chief couldn't search for long. He was busy running away from Crook and his men.

Crazy Horse finally settled upon a site along the Tongue River, but the lack of provisions proved overwhelming. His tribe was suffering from hunger and the frigid temperatures. Many of his people begged him to meet with Miles to ask him what they needed to do to find food and warmth. Crazy Horse did not want to live on a reservation, but he did not stop his people from exploring the possibilities. He accompanied a party of about thirty chiefs to a hill near Fort Keogh, which was named after Captain Myles Keogh, who had been killed at Little Bighorn. From there, eight rode to the fort, including one carrying a white flag. But several Crow Indians whom the soldiers had been using as scouts rode out of the fort and shot at the Sioux, who were forced to ride back to their village. Crazy Horse was certain that now that Miles knew the Sioux were nearby, he would be stalking them yet again.

Sure enough, Miles sent his soldiers out. They tracked down the Sioux camp through foot-deep snow on January 8, 1877. Crazy Horse had little ammunition, but his warrior chiefs led the soldiers into a canyon and kept them at bay during a raging blizzard. Miles soon ordered his troops back to Fort Keogh. But the Sioux also were forced to flee. They rode to the more familiar country of the Little Powder, where they camped in February and managed to survive on the rare game that still existed in the area. Soon they received word that Spotted Tail was on the way. The Brule chief, who had been moved to an agency that bore his name, was planning to convince Crazy Horse to surrender. He had been told by Crook to give Crazy Horse the message that if he yielded peacefully, the reservation to which he would be moved would not be on the Missouri River, where the Sioux hated to live.

Crazy Horse left his camp, but told his father to let Spotted Tail know that his Oglala would come in to the reservation as soon as the weather permitted the transfer of the women and children. Crazy Horse would let his people go if they wished, but he had yet to decide if he would join them. When Spotted Tail arrived to discover that Crazy Horse had vanished, he sent messengers out to find him. On the way back to Nebraska, Spotted Tail convinced a group of Miniconjous led by chief Big Foot to surrender and did the same to several other Sioux chiefs.

Soon it was Red Cloud's turn to try to convince Crazy Horse to come in with a promise from Crook that the latter could have a reservation in the Powder River country. By that time, it seemed Crazy Horse had no choice. His nine hundred Oglala and their horses were starving. They had no ammunition with which to fight. A bitter Crazy Horse finally surrendered at Fort Robinson. Though still respected, even idolized, by his people, the last Sioux war chief was a prisoner of a reservation with no authority despite the fact that the white man had never defeated him in battle.

Late that summer, Crazy Horse was informed that new president Rutherford B. Hayes had invited him to Washington to discuss the promised reservation in the Powder River country. But Crazy Horse declined. He didn't want to end up like what he perceived Red Cloud and Spotted Tail had become after they had visited the Great Father—white men dressed as Indians.

At about that time, the U.S. Army was at war with Chief Joseph and the *Nez Perce* Indians in what is now Idaho. Agency soldiers began recruiting Sioux to scout for them against the Nez Perce, which infuriated Crazy Horse. He told his young warriors not to be bought to spy against their Indian cousins, but many refused to listen. On August 31, when many Sioux donned Bluecoat uniforms and marched off to work for the Army, Crazy Horse became so angry and disgusted that he threatened to take his people out of the reservation and back to Powder River country.

The Death of Crazy Horse

That's all Crook needed to hear. He ordered eight companies of pony soldiers to ride into the camp and arrest Crazy Horse. Duly warned, Crazy Horse, who wasn't certain about the nature of the advance, directed his people to scatter. He then set out alone for the Spotted Tail agency to find protection in the form of old friend Touch-the-Clouds. But the soldiers discovered Crazy Horse there and escorted him back to Fort Robinson to see Crook. He was placed in the custody of Captain James Kensington and an agency policeman whom Crazy Horse recognized. It was Little Big Man, a once brave and defiant Sioux who had fought alongside him against U.S. soldiers and who had at one time threatened to kill the first Sioux who spoke in favor of selling the Black Hills. Now the white man had transformed him into an agency policeman.

Kensington and Little Big Man led Crazy Horse past a soldier named Private William Gentiles into a doorway. Suddenly Crazy Horse lunged away. Little Big Man grabbed him by the arm and the two scuffled briefly. That's when Gentiles plunged his bayonet deep through Crazy Horse's kidneys. The Oglala Sioux chief died that night—September 5, 1877—at the age of thirty-five. The soldiers presented the body to Crazy Horse's parents, who rode it to the Spotted Tail agency, where it was mounted on a scaffold. Throughout that fall, mourners stopped by and gazed at his burial place.

But with Crazy Horse gone, the U.S. government saw no reason to keep its promise of allowing his tribesmen to stay in a reservation at the Powder River. Instead, it was announced they would be forced to leave Nebraska for a new reservation along the barren land of the Missouri River. During that fall, long lines of Indians headed northeast, although several bands peeled off for Canada to join Sitting Bull. Among them were Crazy Horse's mother and father, who carried along with them the decaying body of their son. They buried Crazy Horse somewhere near Chankpe Opi Wakpala, the creek otherwise known as Wounded Knee.

The era of Lakota resistance was essentially over. The same could also be soon said of the Cheyenne. By the spring of 1877, about one hundred thousand Northern Cheyenne had relocated to agencies, including those led by such illustrious chiefs as Dull Knife, Standing Elk, and Little Wolf. They anticipated living on reservations with the Sioux, as was promised them by the Treaty of 1868. But they were in for a rude awakening. They were told instead that they were being sent south to live in Indian Territory with the Southern Cheyenne in what is now Oklahoma. The Northern Cheyenne, who vastly preferred to stay near the Black Hills, met with Crook, who assured them that if they didn't like living in Indian Territory, they would be welcomed back north.

The journey south was made easier by the presence of Army Lieutenant Henry W. Lawton, who was put in charge of the operation. Lawton allowed the old and sick Cheyenne to ride in the soldier wagons and gave the Indians army tents in which to sleep. He made certain they had enough to eat and drink. But the trip was far from pleasant, particularly from an emotional standpoint. As they traversed south, they noticed construction throughout the plains. Railroads and buildings peppered the landscape. Only a few buffalo and antelope herds could be seen. Lawton did provide rifles to thirty warriors who wished to hunt, but that was small consolation.

It took three months for the Northern Cheyenne to reach Fort
Reno on the Cheyenne-Arapaho reservation. They soon discovered to their dismay that there was not enough to eat, very little
game was available for hunting, and the summer heat was intol-
erable. Shortly after their arrival they were invited by the
Southern Cheyenne to a feast traditionally given to newcomers,
but the meal consisted only of watery soup, which was all they
had on hand.

Recalling the promise that his people could return north if they
didn't like their experience, chief Little Wolf approached the
agent and told him they wanted to go back. But the agent replied
that only the President of the United States could allow the
Northern Cheyenne to travel to Black Hills country. He promised
that more food was on the way. He said that a cattle drive through
Texas would soon provide them with plenty of beef. He hadn't
lied; meat was on the way, but it was of poor quality and there
wasn't enough for everyone. By late summer, the Northern Cheyenne began contracting malaria, for which the post doctor had no
quinine to treat. Many of them died from disease and starvation.

The Northern Cheyenne finally received permission from Indian agent John Miles to hunt buffalo, which they were convinced would again make them healthy. Miles enlisted some
Southern Cheyenne to keep an eye on them so they wouldn't
escape back north. But the Northerners discovered to their horror that only piles of buffalo bones remained. White hunters had
slaughtered the animals and left them to rot on the Plains. All
that the Northern Cheyenne could find to kill were coyotes, but
there weren't enough to eat. By the end of the winter, they were
forced to eat all their dogs lest they starve to death.

And when spring came around, swarms of mosquitoes caused
malaria to spread again in the Cheyenne reservation. A measles
epidemic also began killing children. The entire tribe was
threatened with extinction. Little Wolf told Miles that he and
his people couldn't stay another year because he was afraid they
would all be dead. The chiefs, however, were divided. They
believed it would be safer to stay on the reservation than travel
north, where the threat of a slaughter by soldiers seemed quite
real. But Little Wolf and Dull Knife opted for what they believed

to be the lesser of two evils. They informed the 237 men, women, and children in their tribe on September 9, 1878, that they would all be leaving the following morning. Since not enough horses were available to carry them all, they alternated riding and walking. It was a painful blow to a people who a decade earlier owned more horses than any of the Plains tribes. But they rode what they had for three days.

Sure enough, the army caught wind of their travels and tracked them down. But remarkably, considering their distinct lack of numbers, which included fewer than eighty warriors, the Northern Cheyenne held their own. They fought off the soldiers in several skirmishes across Kansas and into Nebraska. They were chased constantly not only by soldiers, but by thrill-seeking cowboys, ranchers, and settlers as well. An estimated ten-thousand soldiers and three thousand other white men joined in at various points, but the plucky Cheyenne who survived the bullets continued to plod their way north, though some peeled off and set new trails. Both the elderly and the children became sick and hungry as winter approached. Dull Knife advised that they seek refuge at Red Cloud's agency, where they could receive food and shelter. After all, they had aided Red Cloud and his people when they were fighting for the Powder River country. Perhaps Red Cloud could return the favor. But Little Wolf would hear none of it. He was heading to the traditional Cheyenne territory along the Tongue River, which he believed to be still fertile with game. He wanted to be a proud and free Cheyenne, again.

They decided to split up. One group, which included children, the elderly, the sick, and only just a few warriors, followed Dull Knife into Red Cloud's agency. The rest accompanied Little Wolf in the march toward the Tongue River. But the former was surrounded by soldiers just a two-day traverse from their destination. The soldiers did not fight them. Rather, the captain informed them that both the Red Cloud and Spotted Tail agencies had been moved north to Dakota. The Northern Cheyenne were offered an opportunity to live at Fort Robinson instead. It was far from Dull Knife's ideal option, but he had had no choice. His fellow Indians were sick, tired, and hungry and the snow had begun to fall. They followed the soldiers to the fort.

The chiefs, however, had not lost all their fighting spirit. That night, they secretly took apart their best guns and placed them underneath the women's clothing. When asked by the soldiers the next morning to disarm, they created a small pile of shoddy guns, as well as some bows and arrows.

Notes

1. Garland, Hamlin. "Two Moon's Story of the Battle: A Cheyenne's account of the Battle of the Little Bighorn." *McClure's Magazine* 11 (1898): 444. http://www.astonisher.com/archives/museum/two_moon_little_big_horn.html

2. Lewis, John E. *The Mammoth Book of Native Americans*. New York: Carroll & Graf Publishers, 2004. 258–59.

3. Brown, Dee. *Bury My Heart at Wounded Knee*. New York: Henry Holt and Company, 1970. 298–99.

4. Hyde, George. *Spotted Tail's Folk: History of the Brule Sioux*. Norman, Oklahoma: University of Oklahoma Press, 1961. 255.

THREE

Beginning of the End

THE NORTHERN CHEYENNE WERE treated well upon their arrival at Fort Robinson, though they were placed in a log barracks that was quite small for their numbers. But at least they had shelter from the cold, as well as blankets, food, and medicine. The soldiers were friendly and helpful.

Dull Knife and his people still yearned to be escorted to Red Cloud's new agency, but were told that only could be achieved through orders from Washington. The fort commander did give them permission to hunt wild game. Though they appreciated the freedom to wander, there was little game left on the prairie and the tipis that once peppered the landscape were gone, which proved quite depressing.

What also proved depressing were the words uttered by Red Cloud, who was beckoned along with American Horse and other Sioux from the Pine Ridge agency in Dakota to speak to the Cheyenne:

> "Our hearts are sore for you," Red Cloud said. "Many of our blood are among your dead. This has made our hearts bad. But what can we do? The Great Father is all-powerful. His people fill the whole earth. We must do what he says. We have begged him to allow you to come to live among us. We hope he may let you come. What we have we will share with you. But remember, what he directs, that you must do. We cannot help you. The snows are thick on the hills. Our ponies are thin. The game is scarce. You cannot resist, nor can we. So listen to your old friend and do without complaint what the Great Father tells you."

> Dull Knife argued that he and his people had done what the Great Father told them to do, which was travel south to Fort Reno, and it

ended in disaster. "We know you for our friend, whose words we may believe," he told Red Cloud. ". . . We bowed to the will of the Great Father and went far into the south where he told us to go. There we found a Cheyenne cannot live. Sickness came among us that made mourning in every lodge. Then the treaty promises were broken, and our rations were short. Those not worn by diseases were wasted by hunger. To stay there meant that all of us would die. Our petitions to the Great Father were unheeded. We thought it better to die fighting to regain our old homes than to perish of sickness. Then our march was begun. The rest you know."[1]

Dull Knife then pleaded with new Fort Robinson commander Henry Wessells, explaining that if he and his people were going to die, then they wished to die on their homeland up north. He guaranteed that they would make no war if they were allowed to stay. But he added that if they were forced to head south again to Fort Reno, they would kill themselves.

His warning either never reached Washington or meant nothing to the War Department, which on January 3, 1879, sent a message stating that the Northern Cheyenne had to return to Fort Reno or the entire Indian reservation system would be in for a shock. General Philip Sheridan ordered that the trek be made immediately—never mind the frigid temperatures and blizzards.

The order was met with defiance. Dull Knife refused to agree to the move, which he believed would have resulted in death to some or all of his people. Wessels replied that the Cheyenne had five days to change their minds—and in the meantime would receive no food or wood for the heating stove.

Wessells was true to his word. The Cheyenne tried to keep warm in the barracks. They had nothing to eat or drink aside from the snow they scraped off the window ledges. Five days later, Wessells returned to order them to prepare for their trek. Wessells left the room, whereupon one of the warriors lifted up the floorboards under which they had stored bits of pieces of the ammunition collected on the way to Fort Robinson. They were to die fighting rather than succumb to the suicidal orders from the Great Father.

Cheyenne Rebellion

The Cheyenne began their revolt the night Wessells issued his ultimatum. They fired shots from their barracks, then raced out, grabbed the rifles from the guards they had wounded with their gunfire and ran to the hills beyond the fort. But they were vastly outnumbered. Soldiers who streamed toward them shot every Indian that moved. The Cheyenne fired back, but within an hour more than half the warriors were dead. The soldiers then began gunning down groups of women and children who scattered about in the deep snow. Those Cheyenne who were not dead were captured and returned to Fort Robinson, but thirty-eight managed to escape and were tracked down again by the soldiers. They were found trapped in a deep rut. The soldiers stood over them and shot at them until there was no return fire. Twenty-nine more Indians were killed. The nine others were taken prisoner. Only six Cheyenne managed to escape captivity through the ordeal. One was Dull Knife, who found his way to Pine Ridge and joined up with Red Cloud on that reservation.

Meanwhile, Lone Wolf and those who elected to join him in traversing to Tongue River country spent the winter hiding from soldiers. When spring arrived, they continued the journey, but soon learned that Lieutenant William F. Clark was seeking them out. The man the Cheyenne called White Hat had grown friendly with Little Wolf and had even asked him to stay with him at Fort Robinson before the decision was made to head south to Fort Reno. Clark indeed found Little Wolf and his tired tribe and disarmed himself to display his peaceful intentions and friendship. White Hat informed the Cheyenne that his orders were to escort them to nearby Fort Keogh, where some of their relatives now lived. Little Wolf told Clark of his people's trials and tribulations over the past year and a half, but felt comforted that the soldier he was dealing with was a friend. Little Wolf turned in his guns.

The Northern Cheyenne were both beat and beaten. Most of the young tribesmen served as scouts. Many became alcoholics from the whisky sold to them by white traders. They drank from boredom and misery. Little Wolf was one who fell into the trap.

Eventually, he and the others were allowed to join Dull Knife and the few who remained alive from that group at Pine Ridge. The spirit of the Northern Cheyenne had been broken.

The Northern Cheyenne had been tamed, but the same could not yet be said of the Sioux, though they had lost the Black Hills and had been pushed out of Nebraska. Their various tribes had been separated into a number of agencies. Red Cloud's Oglala lived in Pine Ridge, Spotted Tail and his Brule were at Rosebud, and others made their homes at Crow Creek, Cheyenne River, and Standing Rock. Even the land separating those reservations was being taken away from the Sioux as settlers continued to swarm though into Dakota. Roads and railroads were built across the Dakota region and shrewd businessmen were conjuring up ways of extracting every last dollar out of the Great Sioux Reservation.

There could be no battle for that land. The Sioux had neither the weapons nor the energy to fight. They struggled merely to feed and clothe themselves. They could draw no inspiration from Sitting Bull, who had taken three thousand Sioux north to Canada. Some in Washington believed it prudent to bring Sitting Bull back to the United States, where he too could be pacified by placement on a reservation.

The result was an arrangement between the War Department and the Canadian government to allow U.S. General Alfred Terry and a special commission to trek over the border under the guidance and protection of the Royal Canadian Mounted Police and speak with Sitting Bull. Terry offered the Hunkpapa chief a complete pardon for his perceived crimes as long as he agreed to turn in all his firearms and horses and bring his people into the Standing Rock agency on the Great Sioux Reservation. He told Sitting Bull that he had ridden hundreds of miles with the message that the U.S. government wanted to live in peace with the Indians, that too much blood had already been shed on both sides, and that all hostilities should cease.

Sitting Bull, who had to be talked into meeting with Terry by Mounted Police Commissioner James MacLeod, had heard such promises spoken before.

"What have we done that you should want us to stop?" Sitting Bull asked Terry. "We have done nothing. It is all the people on your side

that have started us to do all these depredations. We could not go anywhere else, and so we took refuge in this country. . . . I would like to
know why you came here. . . . You come here to tell us lies, but we
don't want to hear them. . . . Don't you say any more words. Go back
home where you came from. The part of the country you gave me you
ran me out of. I have now come here to stay with these people, and I
intend to stay here."[2]

Upon his return to the United States, Terry wrote to the War
Department that the existence of such a large number of Indians
led by Sitting Bull on the northern border of the United States
constituted a threat to the peace of the Indian territories, which
had greatly been subdued. Meanwhile, MacLeod explained to
Sitting Bull that not only would his tribe receive no help from
the Canadians, but that if they crossed the American border
with hostile intent, they would be forced to fight U.S. soldiers
and the Mounted Police.

The attempt at that point to lure Sitting Bull back failed. But
though not attacked as they were in America, the Sioux chief and
his people were unhappy in Canada as well. The winters up north
were even more brutal than they were in the Black Hills and
there was little to hunt. The Canadians were true to their word.
They did not provide food or clothing even in the most brutal
weather. The exodus back to the United States would soon start.

Learning the White World

The white man had taken the land away from the Indians. Now
he would work to remove their tribal identities as well. The effort
to educate the Indians began in the late 1870s in the name of
assimilation. The first off-reservation boarding school to try its
hand at it was the Hampton Institute in Virginia, which had been
concentrating on educating newly freed black slaves. Former missionary Samuel Armstrong, a white man who had led a black regiment during the Civil War, had founded the institution.

The first Indian student body consisted of five Kiowa, eleven
Cheyenne, and one Arapaho, all of whom had been taken into
custody near the Red River during battles on the southern Plains

and had been transferred to Fort Marion in St. Augustine, Florida. At Hampton, the seventeen Indian students were taught to be farmers, ministers, seamstresses, millers, and even lawyers. They were placed into the hands of housefather and renowned black educator and author Booker T. Washington.

Other boarding schools for Indians sprang up in which English was the only language permitted to be spoken. Some students were physically and without permission taken away from their Indian parents. They were taught the Christian religion with a heavy emphasis on Bible reading, their hair was shorn short, and they were forced to wear the clothing of white people. In 1879, the Carlisle Industrial School for Indians in the city that bears its name became the first institution created exclusively for Indians. Missionaries on the Northern Plains had recruited many in its first class. Headmaster Richard Pratt coined the phrase "Kill the Indian and Save the Man" as the school's mission statement.[3] By 1880 more than seven thousand Indian children had been enrolled in boarding schools that were financed by the government and run by missionaries.

Among the Brule Sioux that placed his children in Carlisle was chief Spotted Tail, who withdrew them when he realized that it was working to remove their Indian identities. He did believe that learning to thrive in a white man's world had become a necessity. But he was angered that the Carlisle school was brainwashing his children into rejecting their past. To placate Spotted Tail the Indian Bureau built him a large frame house in which to live near the Rosebud Agency. That infuriated fellow tribesman Crow Dog, who not only didn't like Spotted Tail, but also suspected that he was selling off Lakota land to the railroad companies. Without provocation, Crow Dog shot Spotted Tail dead as the latter rode horseback along a trail. Crow Dog was later convicted of murder, but the U.S. Supreme Court ruled that the court had no jurisdiction over Crow Dog and overturned the conviction.

It was in this climate of Sioux children assimilating to white culture and once-proud warriors and their families either dying off or surviving on government handouts that Sitting Bull returned to the United States. His people in Canada began feeling homesick as 1880 approached; some even crossed the border to surrender to Sioux agencies in Dakota. Sitting Bull might have stayed in Canada had that nation created a reservation on which he and his fellow Sioux could survive. But he was told since they had come from the United States that they had no rights to land. The frigid temperatures in the winter of 1880 killed many of their horses, which forced the Sioux who wished to return to America to travel by foot the following spring. Even the most hardened and proud Sioux such as Gall left Sitting Bull and set out for the Dakota reservation.

Sitting Bull and one hundred eighty-six of his most faithful disciples finally did the same in mid-summer 1881. The Hunkpapa chief escorted his people into Fort Randall, the nearest military outpost, and gave his rifle to his four-year-old son Crow Foot to turn into the commanding officer. Sitting Bull might have looked old and defeated, but he would eventually display the spunk and pride that had made him the most feared Indian warrior on the Plains. His days of fighting soldiers were over; the Indians had neither the ammunition nor the numbers for that anymore. But when the U.S. government forwarded a plan to break up the Great Sioux Reservation in 1882, he led the fight to stop it.

Sitting Bull did not realize what the mere mention of his name meant to his fellow Indians and white America as well when he returned from Canada. He thought he had been forgotten during his stay up north, but quite the opposite was true. He had become a revered leader to chiefs and others on the reservations and a legend in the American media. The slaughter at Little Bighorn was now thought of by most whites as a meaningless event from the distant past. Now that the Indians were no longer a threat, Sitting Bull was still considered a great man in the white world, though albeit a harmless one.

Sitting Bull certainly had something to say to representatives of various Sioux agencies who clamored about to ask him what he thought about the government proposal to sell half the Great Sioux Reservation land for white settlement. Though Sitting Bull knew he no longer had any power, he strongly advised his fellow Indians not to sell, explaining that they simply didn't have enough land of their own. The Sioux heeded his advice and refused to sell.

A U.S. commission decided to try another tactic. It visited a number of agencies and told the Indians that if they signed some papers, they would receive twenty-five thousand cows and one thousand bulls. The Indians couldn't read English and were not told that in return for the cattle, they must surrender fourteen thousand square miles of territory. The methods used to secure the signatures were highly questionable, even to many in Washington, who pointed out that according to earlier treaties, three-fourths of all adult male Sioux needed to sign. And that wasn't about to happen. The commissioner had even tricked Indian boys as young as seven years old to affix their signatures upon the document.

The ploy used by the commission was shady enough to motivate another commission, this one led by Senator Henry L. Dawes, to head to the reservations to investigate. By the time the commissioners arrived at the Standing Rock agency, Sitting Bull had been released from custody at the military fort and was living there with his fellow Hunkpapa Sioux. It was then Sitting Bull showed the influence he could still exert over his fellow tribesmen. When asked his view of the situation, Sitting Bull spoke derisively of Dawes and his commissioners, motioned to his fellow Indians, and walked from the room. Every last Sioux followed him out, leaving the commissioners to themselves.

Sitting Bull was confronted by other Hunkpapa leaders that afternoon who told him that though they remained loyal to him, he should understand that the Dawes commission was on their side in the fight to keep their land. Sitting Bull distrusted all whites, but he was determined to apologize for leading his fellow Sioux out of the room. When the Indians met with the commission later that day, he was prepared to do just that, but after speaking at length about how he was willing to accept the ways of the white man because the American government had promised peace and prosperity, he was verbally attacked by Senator John Logan.

"I want to say that further you are not a great chief of this country," Logan said. "That you have no following, no power, no control. You are on an Indian reservation merely at the sufferance of the government. You are fed by the government, clothed by the government, your children are educated by the government, and all you have and are today is because of the government. If it were not for the government you would be freezing and starving today in the mountains. I merely say these things to notify you that you cannot insult the people of the United States of America or its committees. . . . The government feeds and clothes and educates your children now, and desires to teach you to become farmers, and to civilize you, and make you as white men."[4]

McLaughlin was trusted by most of the Sioux; he even had a Santee wife. But McLaughlin was also instructed to do everything in his power to take the power out of Sitting Bull's hands, so he worked with Gall on matters of importance. The tactic failed; the Hunkpapa still idolized Sitting Bull.

So, in fact, did much of America. When the Northern Pacific Railroad celebrated the completion of its transcontinental track in September 1883, officials with the company decided that Sitting Bull would be an ideal candidate to speak at the ceremony in Bismarck, North Dakota His words were to be translated to the crowd by a young army officer, who was also assigned to help Sitting Bull prepare the speech. All seemed well when Sitting Bull and the Bluecoat arrived on that late summer day. But when the Sioux chief began his speech in his native language, the translator listened incredulously.

"I hate all the white people," he began. "You are thieves and liars. You have taken away our land and made us outcasts."[5]

Sitting Bull knew that only the translator could understand his words, so he appeared to be graciously accepting the occasional applause, then bowed and smiled before lashing out again to the adoring crowd. Upon the conclusion of the speech, the shaken translator walked to the podium and read the kind words from the prepared text, which included flowery prose about how happy Sitting Bull was to be there and how he eagerly awaited the days when the Indian and white man could live together in harmony and prosperity, prompting the crowd to give Sitting Bull a standing ovation. The Hunkpapa chief was cheered so wildly that the railroad officials invited him to speak at an upcoming ceremony in Minnesota. The U.S. Secretary of the Interior soon authorized for Sitting Bull a tour of fifteen American cities.

Despite his hatred and mistrust of white people, Sitting Bull accepted the invitation. He was embraced by the same white people in his appearances, which were met with such enthusiasm that William (Buffalo Bill) Cody came up with a brainstorm: he would add Sitting Bull to his touring Wild West Show. The Indian Bureau was skeptical of the plan at first, but it seemed more appealing upon deeper study. After all, the Bureau reasoned, Sitting Bull remained a threat, or at least a revered leader to his fellow Sioux when he was in their midst. But off the reservation, as the lone Indian among thousands of white people, he would be harmless. The more Standing Rock head McLaughlin thought about it, the more he came to believe that convincing the Sioux to blend into white society would be a far easier task with Sitting Bull out of the way.

That line of thinking certainly benefited Buffalo Bill Cody and his Wild West Show, which proved hugely successful beginning in the summer of 1885 with Sitting Bull as an attraction. It toured the United States and Canada and, though some booed the Sioux chief for his role in the Battle of the Little Bighorn, most cheered. Further, the same fans who screamed at him derisively often joined other patrons in lining up to grab copies of his autographed photo. Sitting Bull had little interest in the money being paid him; in fact, he gave much of it away to poor white boys in raggedy clothes who streamed out in droves to see him. He grew worrisome and angry over the discrepancies in financial standing among white people. Sitting Bull even told sharpshooter Annie Oakley, who was also part of the show, that white men knew how to make money and goods, but they didn't know how to distribute them fairly. He did, however, feel an appreciation for Cody, to whom he gave a large white sombrero and a horse that had been trained to sit, as well as raise a hoof at the sound of a gunshot.

Sitting Bull and Buffalo Bill

Two years later, Buffalo Bill offered him a spot in the show, this time on a tour of Europe. But Sitting Bull declined the opportunity in the belief that the U.S. government was again formulating a plan to take land away from the Indians and that he was needed back at the reservation.

He was prophetic, though the new plan wasn't a land grab. It was created by Dawes, whose goal was to turn the Indians into land-owning farmers, and it became known as the General Allot-ment Act, Dawes Act, and Homestead Act. The Senate passed the bill, which allowed the heads of Indian families the opportu-nity to apply for allotments of 160 acres on reservation farm-land. Single adult men would receive half that while miners would be allowed 40 acres. Acreage double the size of the farm-land would be provided for those who required grazing territory. The Indians who didn't apply for land would be given land by the government after four years. And after a quarter-century of working the land, the Indian families would be given ownership of it. Any land left over after the plan played itself out would be sold to settlers.

The Dawes Act was popular even among those in the business of protecting and forwarding Indian rights and nudging them down the path of civilization. Individual Indians, rather than entire tribes, would now own their own land, on which they would learn to become farmers.

In 1888, Congress passed the Sioux Act, which turned the Dawes Act into law for those living on the Great Sioux Reserva-tion, including the Oglala and Brule just north of what is now the border between Nebraska and South Dakota, the Miniconjou west of the Missouri River, the Hunkpapa at Standing Rock, which bor-dered North Dakota and South Dakota, and other scattered bands such as the Itazipacola, Oohenunpa, and Sihasapa. The government estimated from Sioux population numbers that after all the Indians had been provided farm land, about half their res-ervation, totaling about ten million acres, could be considered sur-plus and sold to settlers. Much of the money earned from those settlers would be placed into interest-bearing accounts to pay for Indian educational programs and would also pay for livestock and farming equipment for the Sioux.

It appeared on the surface to be a step forward for the Sioux, particularly considering their circumstances at the time. But there were drawbacks, including the fact that they objected to not receiving all their land, which in the future could be used to house their children. They also objected to the government proposing to buy the land at fifty cents an acre and selling it back for one dollar and twenty-five cents an acre. The result was that only twenty-two Sioux at Standing Rock signed the proposal, which didn't fare much better at the other agencies either.

More than sixty Lakota Sioux chiefs were included in a delegation sent to the Secretary of the Interior to voice their concerns. The Congress negotiated with them before finalizing the Sioux Act of 1889, which stipulated that the Sioux would receive one dollar and twenty-five cents for every acre sold to settlers during the first three years after enactment of the new law. Since the best land would be purchased during that time, the Act also stipulated that land would be sold for seventy-five cents an acre in the fourth and fifth years and fifty cents thereafter. The bill also doubled the amount of land provided heads of Indian families and increased financing for improving the land. The government even offered to survey all the borders surrounding the various agencies in the Great Sioux Reservation to safeguard individual Indian property. It would also find new property for Sioux who currently lived on land sold to settlers.

The negotiations were headed by General George Crook—the same George Crook who had fought the Sioux and Cheyenne more than a decade earlier. But Crook had done an about-face in his dealing with Indians. He had learned from them and had advocated for fairer treatment. He had sided with Geronimo and the Apache Indians during negotiations in Arizona in 1882 after having realized that their complaints against Indian agencies were valid. Crook ordered that all miners and squatters be removed from their reservation. He also made certain that rations were plentiful, kept soldiers from harassing them, and convinced the Army to buy all their vegetable crops.

It was indeed a changed George Crook who arrived in May 1889 to the Great Sioux Reservation. He had plenty of convincing to do. Respected chiefs such as Sitting Bull, Red Cloud, Little Wound, Young-Man-Afraid-of-His-Horses, and Big Road all opposed the agreement. His first stop was to the Rosebud Agency to try to convince the Brules to sign. The murder of

Spotted Tail had split that tribe into factions, but tribesmen such as Hollow Horn Bear, High Hawk, and Yellow Hair refused, claiming that there would not be enough land for their descendants. Crook then issued a warning that they had heard many times before.

> "The white men in the east are like birds," he told them. "They are hatching out their eggs every year, and there is not enough room in the East and they must go elsewhere; and they come west, as you have seen them coming for the last few years. And they are still coming, and will come until they overrun all of this country; and you can't prevent it. . . . Everything is decided in Washington by the majority, and these people come out west and see that the Indians have a big body of land they are not using and they say 'we want that land.' "[6]

The Brule eventually softened and the majority signed after more than a week of discussion. The first to affix his signature on the document was Crow Dog, the assassin of Spotted Tail.

Crook moved on to negotiate with Red Cloud and his Oglala at Pine Ridge. Red Cloud was far more defiant, surrounding the commissioners with several hundred mounted warriors. Crook's men did manage to convince about half the Oglala to sign, but mindful that the Treaty of 1868 required that three-fourths of all adult male Indians needed to agree for a bill to become law, the commissioners moved on to what they hoped would be more willing Sioux in the smaller agencies. Those trips proved quite fruitful as they received signatures of the vast majority of the Sioux at Lower Brule, Crow Creek, and Cheyenne River. The sternest test, however, wouldn't be met until July 27, 1889. That's when Crook and his commissioners arrived to meet with Sitting Bull and his Hunkpapa tribe, as well as some Blackfoot Sioux, at the Standing Rock agency. Sitting Bull urged his people to stand firm against the sale of land to whites or fellow Indians and the traditionalists of the tribe agreed, but others leaned toward accepting the new terms. Crook spoke to them, but got nowhere. After a few days, he warned the Oglala and Blackfoot that if they didn't sign the agreement, the government would simply take their land without compensation. Considering past negotiations with the United States, the Indians were duly frightened. Crook then enlisted the help of Standing Rock agent James McLaughlin to convince individual Sioux that indeed Crook's warning was not merely talk. But Sitting Bull refused to budge, arguing that the Indians shouldn't sell their land simply to save the government the embarrassment of stealing land by breaking the terms of the Treaty of 1868.

McLaughlin decided nothing could be achieved if Sitting Bull remained an influence, so the Sioux chief was not invited to a meeting with the commissioners on August 3, 1889. Sitting Bull, however, learned of the meeting and entered the council circle. He asked to speak, whereupon Crook inquired of McLaughlin about whether Sitting Bull had been informed of the meeting. McLaughlin lied, answering that the Sioux chief indeed had been invited.

The commissioners wasted no time after Sitting Bull entered the room. They moved quickly to garner as many signatures as possible and enjoyed great success. Even the one-time bitterly defiant Gall signed. They now had the required three-quarters of the Indians on board. The Great Sioux Reservation would be broken up and white immigrants would soon be flooding in to the land Sitting Bull believed the Great Spirit had given to his people. When a reporter asked him how the Indians felt about surrendering their land, a sickened and angry Sitting Bull responded with a line that has become legend in the history of Indian relations: "Indians! There are no more Indians left but me!"[7]

Sitting Bull's skepticism in regard to the intentions of the U.S. government proved justified, though statistical analyses and poor participation in the process of some Sioux played a role in the Indians not receiving all that was promised. Shortly after the agreement became official, the beef ration was halved. The government counted fewer Indians than anticipated, because some simply didn't cooperate with census takers. Beef rations on Pine Ridge alone were sliced by about one million pounds a year.

Further violations of the land sale, however, could not be blamed on the Sioux, including President William Henry Harrison's declaration in early 1890 that the surplus land would be opened to settlers immediately rather than waiting for the surveying process to protect the rights of Indians already living on it. The result of the land sale and breakup of the reservation was further splintering of the Indians, many of whom could no longer ride exclusively on reservation territory to visit family and friends. And to traverse on land occupied by settlers, the Indians were forced to apply for special permits.

Losing All Hope

The Sioux fell into utter despair. Even those who held a strong sense of optimism upon the signing of the agreement lost all hope. They were hungry, angry, and thoroughly defeated. Another slap in the face occurred in late 1889 when South Dakota was granted statehood, thereby giving whites hungry for land a stronger voice in Congress. One Indian exclaimed bitterly about the whites, "They made us many promises, more than I can remember, but they never kept but one; they promised to take our land, and they took it."[8]

The plight of the Lakota soon worsened. Those who attended the discussions regarding land allotment returned to find their livestock stolen or killed. Outbreaks of whooping cough and measles sent many children to an early grave. Such diseases killed an average of forty-five Sioux per month in 1889. Even former Indian fighter General Nelson Miles decried the disease and starvation prevalent on the reservations, as well as the fact that they had not been paid for the surrendered territory.

But aside from a few dissenters, who was fighting for a Sioux people that could no longer fight for themselves? Red Cloud later asked that very question in a note to a white friend.

> "How can we eat or waste what we have not?" he wrote. "We felt that we were mocked in our misery. We had no newspapers, and no one to speak for us. We had no redress. Our rations were again reduced. You, who eat three times a day and see your children well and happy around you, can't understand what starving Indians feel. We were faint with hunger and maddened by despair. We held our dying children and felt their little bodies tremble as their souls went out and left only a

dead weight in our hands. . . . There was no hope on earth, and God seemed to have forgotten us."[9]

So did many in the government. Dawes, who authored the plan that bore his name, told Congress that that very body of the government had been encouraged for years to force the Indians into becoming farmers by decreasing their rations on a continual basis, thereby starving them into self-sufficiency. An Indian Department proposal that the rations be diminished annually was even enacted into law. What was conveniently discounted or ignored was that the rations were not a handout. Rather, they were payment for land the Indians sold to the government.

In addition, a severe drought that struck the Dakota Territory in the late 1880s precluded the Indians, who had no background as farmers, from growing crops successfully. They prepared the ground and planted the seeds at the right times, but virtually nothing was harvested. Standing Rock agent James McLaughlin noted that from August 1890 to June 1891 there was no rainfall and little snowfall recorded in the area. He estimated that only one-third to one-half of the oat, wheat, corn, and other vegetable crops could be harvested. And he gave an even darker assessment about the farming situation at Pine Ridge, where the drought destroyed nearly the entire corn crop after a year in which all the vegetables perished from a lack of rain. Yet the rations continued to be cut. Forty percent of the Lakota population had succumbed to disease and starvation in the fourteen years that followed the Battle of the Little Bighorn.

White settlers too suffered from poor crop yield as a result of the drought, but thousands simply packed their bags and headed elsewhere. The Indians, on the other hand, were not allowed to leave their reservations and certainly weren't welcomed in the white working world. Some became desperate and began to steal. Miles wasn't the only former Indian fighter who had come to realize how poorly they were being treated. Another was Colonel Richard I. Dodge, an army officer who had once fought against the Lakota.

"A few years ago," he wrote, "the Indian was wild, free, and independent. Now he is a prisoner of war, restrained of his liberty and confined on circumscribed areas. But a few years ago, the Plains furnished him an ample supply of food; now he is constantly on the verge of starvation. We leave our helpless prisoners to starve, and shoot without mercy the reckless few who, goaded to desperation by their sufferings, dare to cross the dead line of the reservation. In this horrid crime every voter of the United States is either actively or passively implicated, for it has its roots in the legislative branch of the government."[10]

Meanwhile, the implementation of the agreement that was supposed to guarantee land for individual Indians became stalled in bureaucratic red tape. They were unaware of the complexities of the American system, in which decisions were often not finalized for years. Nine months after Crook left the Great Sioux Reservation with enough signatures to push the bill through, the Senate finally passed the bill under Crook's watchful eye. It appeared the promises of the commissioners to the Sioux people were finally to be kept, but it struggled to get through the House of Representatives. And when it did finally become law, the lack of properly conducted surveying had the Indians guessing which land they owned while white settlers poured in from the east. By that time, the beef allowance provided to feed those on the now fragmented Great Sioux Reservation had been reduced to one million pounds, less than one-third of what had been promised in the 1877 treaty.

Soon the vast majority of the Sioux who signed the agreement came under ridicule by those who had stood by their convictions and refused to do so. But there was nothing any of them could do about their misery. They were sick, hungry, outnumbered, and militarily overwhelmed. They were desperate for salvation. And in 1890, a Paiute medicine man named Wovoka delivered hope.

Notes

1. Bronson, Edgar B. *Reminiscences of a Ranchman.* New York: McClure Company, 1908. 167–69 [accessed August 2009]. http://books.google.com/books?id=YA8TAAAAYAAJ&pg=PA167&dq=Reminiscences+of+a+Ranchman:+%22Our+hearts+are+sore+for+you%22#v=onepage&q=&f=false

2. Brown, Dee. *Bury My Heart at Wounded Knee.* New York: Henry Holt and Company, 1970. 418.

3. Nies, Judith. *Native American History*. New York: Ballantine Books, 1996. 291.

4. Paul, Daniel N. We Were Not Savages: First Nation History [accessed August 2009]. http://www.danielnpaul.com/ChiefSittingBull-LakotaNation.html

5. White, Phillip M. *American Indian Chronology: Chronology of the American Mosaic*. Santa Barbara, Calif.: Greenwood Press, 2006. 91.

6. Crook, George. *General George Crook: His Autobiography*. Norman, Oklahoma: University of Oklahoma Press, reprint 1986. 291 [accessed September 2009]. http://books.google.com/books?id=wYRKWd1ORqgC&pg=PP1&dq=General+George+Crook:+His+autobiography#v=one page&q=&f=false

7. Bridger, Bobby. *Buffalo Bill and Sitting Bull: Inventing the Wild West*. Austin, Texas: University of Texas Press, 2002. 374 [accessed September 2009]. http://books.google.com/books?id=twncduiz3WoC&pg=PA374&lpg=PA374&dq=Sitting+Bull:+%22There+are+no+Indians+left+but+me!%22&source=bl&ots=QiHNs0qkor&sig=auERg0XmLZjppPOcmm7MaJc qhGw&hl=en&ei=AyaYSqCSJ5HeMeXd5LIF&sa=X&oi=book_result&ct=result&resnum=7#v=onepage&q=Sitting%20Bull%3A%20%22There%20are%20no%20Indians%20left%20but%20me!%22&f=false

8. Di Silvestro, Roger L. *In The Shadow of Wounded Knee*. New York: Walker and Company, 2005. 62.

9. De Barthe, Joseph. *Life and Adventures of Frank Grouard*. Englewood Cliffs, N.J.: Silver Burdett Press, 1982. 472.

10. Coleman, William S.E. *Voices of Wounded Knee*. Lincoln, Nebraska: University of Nebraska Press, 2000. 20.

FOUR

The Ghost Dance

THE SIOUX FED OFF A deep spirituality and oneness with nature. They believed that the Great Spirit blessed particular holy men they termed *wicasa wakan* with supernatural powers. Among them was Sitting Bull, who felt he could speak to birds and envision the future. His fellow Hunkpapa were also convinced that their chief had been so endowed.

By 1890, however, many Sioux harbored tremendous doubts that the Great Spirit was still looking after them. Their numbers were dwindling as a result of disease and starvation. Hope had given way to misery and dark, grim reality. But that year their deep-rooted belief that Indian holy men could foretell coming events led to a spiritual reawakening. It also led to the bloodiest massacre in American history, one that practically ended all Indian resistance as the nineteenth century faded out.

Experience with those perceived as saviors was not new to the Indian people. In 1805, a Shawnee dreamed that most Indians were doomed to a place much like hell after they died, so he urged them to give up all temptation provided them by whites such as whisky and all livestock aside from horses. He called upon them to eschew clothing worn by white America as well and return to native wear and ornamentation, which included painted faces for men. The man the Shawnee simply called "The Prophet" also told his people to give up all warlike thoughts and intentions and to treat everyone nicely. The Prophet, who said an entity he called the "Great Mystery" led him to these conclusions, added that following on the path set by white people to hunt commercially for animal skins only must also be stopped.

He warned that future hunting must only be done to feed and clothe the Shawnee people. The Great Mystery even told The Prophet that the sap yielded by maple trees must be used solely to help feed the Indians and not sold to whites because that would result in the destruction of too much of the woodlands.

It has been speculated that The Prophet had gained a perception of his god-given abilities through the teachings of a Delaware Indian named Neolin, who had prophesized that the white man would be destroyed by spiritual powers. Neolin had lived among the Shawnee in 1764. A number of native spiritualists had inhabited tribal lands in the east during the second half of the eighteenth century.

None, however, elicited the strength of passion as did Wovoka, who was known to white friends as Jack Wilson. The seeds of his place in history were planted during a solar eclipse on New Year's Day 1889, when he became sick as he chopped wood in a Nevada desert near Pyramid Lake. He went to his domed residence that had been constructed of shrub branches when delirium set in. He fell into a trance and envisioned himself speaking with God and Jesus, who informed him that they were angry with how the white man had killed the latter the last time he had visited Earth. God told Wovoka that He was going to eliminate the white man from the continent by the following spring, resurrect all the dead Indians and the dead wildlife, which would allow the Indians to live in peace, prosperity, and joy again on their native lands. God added that the Indians must surrender all white materials and customs, but treat their people well. He showed Wovoka a special dance that was called the Ghost Dance because it would bring dead Indians back to life. The Paiute medicine man was promised that if he taught his people the Ghost Dance, they would thrive as they did before the white trespassers ruined their way of life.

Thus inspired, Wovoka went off to preach the new religion to tribes near and far. Most of his fellow Indians believed strongly in his power, though not all of them took his preaching at face value. In fact, Southwest tribes such as the Hopi and Navajo ignored the word of Wovoka and the Ghost Dance. But in the autumn of 1889, the Lakota became intrigued enough to send eleven representatives on a 1,400-mile trek to Nevada to learn about it. The delegation returned several months later with details of the Ghost Dance and its supposed miraculous benefits. Wovoka and those whom he taught it also spread the word to Indians throughout the West.

Among the first of the sixteen tribes represented in Nevada that embraced the Ghost Dance was chief Big Foot's Miniconjou Lakota, who resided on the Cheyenne River Reservation. The Miniconjou were particularly independent, as well as distrustful of and angry with U.S. government policies, all of which resulted in an acceptance of the Ghost Dance as salvation. By the end of the summer of 1890, the Miniconjou and other tribes were danc- ing, sometimes for days on end, to the point of exhaustion. Whites didn't know what to make of it, but they tended to fear the worst. Despite the fact that Big Foot had just four hundred followers, most of whom were women and children, and was in ill-health, some believed that the mysterious dance was a pre- cursor to an attack. Troops from Fort Meade, led by Captain A.J. Henissee, were dispatched. They camped close to the reservation and sent soldiers to observe, but the situation remained peace- ful. In fact, the soldiers played games and had races with the Miniconjou children and some even danced with them near summer's end. Henissee informed Big Foot's people to limit the Ghost Dancing to Saturdays, which they readily agreed to do. Yet Big Foot still decided to move away from the reservation. His band spent much of the fall hunting antelope around the Lit- tle Missouri River in North Dakota, turning down invitations from Red Cloud, Afraid-of-His-Horses, and others to join them at the Pine Ridge agency. The hunt was successful enough to pro- vide the Miniconjou enough dried meat to last them through the winter. But upon returning to the reservation, Big Foot began considering the invitation from Pine Ridge.

The misery being experienced on the Sioux reservation moti- vated the Lakota to welcome any possibility for salvation. And what would appear to be a mystical and even absurd shot in the dark to whites was met with tremendous enthusiasm to the des- perate Indians. Among them were Kicking Bear and Short Bull, who had traversed to Nevada to learn the Ghost Dance. Kicking Bear was particularly eager to teach it to his fellow Sioux.

A close friend of Crazy Horse, he had been a fierce warrior in his younger days, having distinguished himself in many battles, including Little Bighorn. His hatred for white people was pronounced. Kicking Bear, who featured a mystical side, felt angry for the pathetic existence that he believed had been imposed upon his people. Short Bull was a Brule medicine man admired for his generosity and good nature who, like Kicking Bear, had also proven himself on the fields of battle. He too was a native traditionalist who would have been quite joyful at seeing the old ways of life returned to the Sioux people.

But just as messages are altered when they bounce from one person to the next, such was the case with the Ghost Dance. Kicking Bear and Short Bull both claimed that the Great Mystery had informed them in dreams that if whites engaged in gun battles with the Lakota, only the gunpowder of the latter would work. Kicking Bear took it a step further, creating the notion that if his people wore ghost shirts, they would be bulletproof. Upon hearing of the alterations to his Ghost Dance practices and philosophy, Wovoka responded that they were not an intended part of the religion. But the Lakota had always been prideful of their sense of independence and were going to believe what they wished.

Kicking Bear at Standing Rock

The Sioux that had investigated Wovoka and the Ghost Dance stopped first at the Pine Ridge Reservation to preach the new religion, though Short Bull played the role of messenger and instructor at Rosebud. He and fellow disciple Good Thunder were undeterred when warned by Indian agents to cease their activities. Kicking Bear found little resistance from officials at the Cheyenne River Reservation. That fall a skeptical Sitting Bull, who didn't believe that the dead could be brought back to life, invited Kicking Bear to Standing Rock. Before being forced off the reservation by the agent, Kicking Bear spoke with great conviction about the Ghost Dance and how it could bring about a return to the Sioux glory days, referring to Jesus in the process.

"My brothers," he began, "I bring to you the promise of a day in which there will be no white man to lay his hand on the bridle of the Indian's horse; when the red man of the prairie will rule the world and not be turned from the hunting-grounds by any man. I bring you word from your fathers the ghosts, that they are now marching to join you, led by the Messiah, who came once to live on earth with the white man, but was cast out and killed by them. I have seen the wonders of the spirit-land and have talked with the ghosts. I have traveled far and am sent back with a message to tell you to make ready for the coming of the Messiah and return of the ghosts in the spring.[1]

How was Kicking Bear certain that the Ghost Dance would produce the desired results? He had heard it directly from the Great Spirit, who had told him:

"I have neglected the Indians for many moons, but I will make them my people now if they obey me in this message. The Earth is getting old, but I will make it new for my chosen people, the Indians, who are to inhabit it, and among them will be all those of their ancestors who have died, their fathers, mothers, brothers, cousins and wives—of those who hear my voice and my words through the tongues of my children. I will cover the Earth with new soil to a depth of five times the height of a man, and under this new soil will be buried the whites, and all the holes and the rotten places will be filled up. The new lands will be covered with sweet-grass and running water and trees, and herds of buffalo and ponies will stray over it that my red children may eat and drink, hunt and rejoice. And the sea to the west I will fill up that no ships may pass over it, and the other seas I will make impassable. . . . Go then, my children, and tell these things to all the people and make all ready for the coming of the ghosts."[2]

Standing Rock agent James McLaughlin grew fearful enough of Kicking Bear to call out a party of thirteen policemen to have him removed from the premises and arrest him. They arrived to find Kicking Bear and Sitting Bull conducting a seance. The officer in charge, however, became so impressed with the stories told by the Indians and the dance that they left without following through on their orders. They feared Kicking Bear's powers, so McLaughlin sent another contingent of officers in to have him removed.

Among the witnesses to the proceedings was a white New Yorker named Catherine Weldon, who represented the National

Indian Defense Association. She had first been sent to Standing Rock in 1888 and had returned in each of the next two years. She became close to Sitting Bull, though whether their relationship had grown to become romantic remains speculative. Weldon hoped to convince Sitting Bull to reject the Ghost Dance, fearing that it would lead to white backlash and get him killed. Both she and Sitting Bull knew quite well that McLaughlin was seeking an excuse to arrest him and that the dance could provide one. After all, the federal government in 1883 had banned religious rituals on Indian reservations. But Sitting Bull saw no potential harm in the Ghost Dance. Though he remained quite skeptical of its power, he believed that if Wovoka and Kicking Bear were accurate in their claims, his people should perform it with passion. And if the dance bore no fruit, what was the harm?

Weldon, however, knew that McLaughlin feared that the dance could stir up violence among the Hunkpapa Sioux. Weldon begged him to disregard that Sitting Bull was allowing the Ghost Dance, claiming that the blame should be placed on Kicking Bear, whom she regarded as evil. She added that if McLaughlin took pity on Sitting Bull and didn't have him arrested, she would bring the chief to him. Weldon attempted to convince Sitting Bull to stop the dancing, but to no avail. Fearing for her own safety, she returned to New York in November 1890. She wrote Sitting Bull that he had been deceived by Kicking Bear and others who had attempted to convince him and his tribe of the validity of the Ghost Dance. She was not the only one who tried to persuade the Hunkpapa chief to abide by the white man's rule. Even his brother-in-law Gray Eagle urged him to do so, but his words were ignored. Sitting Bull didn't believe in the promises of the Ghost Dance, but if he was going to die, he was going to die with defiance against the white man. Gray Eagle replied that the refusal to obey was going to cost Sitting Bull and other Indians their lives. Furthermore, it was going to end their friendship.

McLaughlin called the dance "demoralizing, indecent and disgusting," adding that it was an "absurd craze."[3] The ritual in its basic form consisted of a Paiute round dance in which the Indian men and women formed a circle hand-in-hand and stepped to the left. The Lakota added elements of their own traditional religious rituals, including the placing in the middle of the circle a tree or pole decorated with sacrifices to God. The dancers looked toward the sun, which indicated that they were seeking the aid of the Great Spirit rather than motivation toward violent retribution against the white man. Yet even after McLaughlin witnessed the Ghost Dance first-hand, he continued to claim its dangers. Missionary Mary Collins, another who watched the Lakota perform it, offered her view that it was merely a variation of their Sun Dance. According to one Pine Ridge Agency employee, the costumes were made of white cotton cloth. The women's dresses featured wide, flowing sleeves with feathers hanging off. They were painted blue in the neck and were replete with mystical symbols such as moons, stars, and birds. The men's ghost shirts were made of the same material and were similarly colored, though with added symbols such as bows, arrows, and suns. Though other Plains tribes were dancing and wore such shirts, only the Lakota believed that the garments were bulletproof.

Though the Ghost Dance was being performed in far greater numbers around other reservations, including an estimated six hundred of Big Foot's followers at Cheyenne River, Sitting Bull remained under the greatest suspicion, due greatly to McLaughlin's hatred and mistrust of him. The agent described the Hunkpapa chief as the primary mischief-maker at his agency and added that the Ghost Dance would have died a quiet death if not for his encouragement. McLaughlin complained that the shrinking of attendance at agency schools that taught Christianity and various white ways coincided with the intensity and frequency of Ghost Dancing.

First-hand View of the Ghost Dance

He was ordered to meet with Sitting Bull, which he did in November 1890. In his report to acting Indian Commissioner Robert V. Belt, he stated that upon his arrival about two hundred Sioux, were performing the Ghost Dance in the middle of the camp. He described a woman fainting, after which it was announced by tribesman Bull Ghost that she was in a trance. McLaughlin went on to report that the Indians then stopped dancing and awaited word from the spirit world from the squaw.

"Sitting Bull performed certain incantations, then leaned over to put his ear to the woman's lips," wrote a skeptical McLaughlin. "He spoke in a low voice to his herald, Bull Ghost, who repeated to the listening multitude the message which Sitting Bull pretended to receive from the unconscious woman. The excitement was very intense, the people being brought to a pitch of high nervousness by this treatment prescribed by Sitting Bull for his followers. . . . I did not attempt to stop the dance then going on, as, in their crazed condition under the excitement, it would have been useless to attempt it."[4]

What McLaughlin did attempt later was to speak with the chief directly. He claimed that the moment he warned Sitting Bull that the Ghost Dance was causing trouble, he could see in the eyes of the Hunkpapa leader that he didn't believe in it either. McLaughlin then addressed Sitting Bull's followers, uttering a number of well-worn perceptions of history, such as how the government showed great forgiveness of past Indian crimes, how it saved the Sioux from starvation by allowing them to surrender as prisoners of war a decade earlier and how it had done their children a favor by giving them an education in the ways of the white man. McLaughlin added that he came away believing that his speech had convinced many to shun the Ghost Dance. He also asserted that Sitting Bull admitted the truth of his words and that he believed McLaughlin to be a friend to the Sioux people. Finally, McLaughlin declared that Sitting Bull offered to escort him around to all the reservations, whereupon if they saw no proof that the promise of the Ghost Dance had been delivered, the chief would call an end to it. McLaughlin wrote that he declined, but did invite Sitting Bull to a face-to-face meeting in which he would attempt to convince the Hunkpapa leader of the absurdity and foolishness of the dance craze. That offer too was in vain. Little did McLaughlin know as he left the camp that he would never again see Sitting Bull alive.

McLaughlin concluded his correspondence to Belt by claiming that the Ghost Dance was losing its attraction to many of the Indians and that the coming of winter would slow it down further, leaving Sitting Bull with few adherents. He claimed confidence that he could non-violently end what he derisively called the nonsensical activity in short order. But Belt surprisingly replied that McLaughlin should consider arresting those encouraging the Ghost Dance and that military aid would be available. McLaughlin dutifully wired back several times, but again urged that arrests not be made. And, indeed, a report in the *Chicago Tribune* on November 22 stated that his visit to Standing Rock served to stop the dancing at least temporarily.

Such was not the case, however, at Pine Ridge, where a conflict over the attempted arrest for cattle theft of an Oglala Ghost Dancer named Little erupted into violence. Settlers who lived far beyond the reservation planted the seeds of that violence. Frightened by reports that misinterpreted the Ghost Dance as a precursor to an attack, the frontier people of North Dakota, South Dakota, Nebraska, and Iowa began to panic. Many fled their ranches and homes for the safety of bigger cities, concocting stories along the way about Indian scalping and murder that had no basis in truth.

The problems were exacerbated when an inexperienced pharmacist named Daniel Royer was selected as the new Pine Ridge agent. He knew nothing about Indian agencies, the Sioux people, or the Ghost Dance; his appointment by new South Dakota Senator Richard Pettigrew was based on the fact that he had helped him get elected. Upon his arrival at Pine Ridge, the inhabitants immediately and mockingly named him Young Man Afraid of His Indians. Royer was fearful of the Ghost Dance and called for troops to intervene.

Many progressive Indian leaders and white representatives, such as Pine Ridge doctor and Santee Charles Eastman, superintendent of reservation schools Elaine Goodale, and Oglala Lakota American Horse, attempted to allay Royer's fears by explaining that if he just ignored the Ghost Dance, the practice would die out when it was realized that the whites were not disappearing and the dead Indians were not reviving. But he panicked on November 11, 1890, when Little fought back against Indian police with a knife as he was being arrested for cattle theft. The incident, which occurred in Royer's office, escalated into a dangerous and potentially deadly situation when about two hundred Lakota armed with guns and knives surrounded the police and took them hostage. That's when American Horse stepped in to avert catastrophe.

> "Stop! Think!" he cried out. "What are you going to do? Kill these men of our own race? Then what? Kill all these helpless white men, women and children? And what then? What will these brave words, brave deeds lead to in the end? How long can you hold out? Your country is surrounded with a network of railroads. Thousands of white soldiers will be here within three days. What ammunition have you? What provisions? What will become of your families? Think, think, my brothers. This is a child's madness."[5]

Jack Red Cloud, son of the legendary chief, placed his revolver to the face of American Horse. But the latter remained calm, ignoring the threat on his life, and walked into Royer's office. The mob dispersed, thereby at least temporarily quelling the threat.

The incident, however, only served to heighten Royer's fears, particularly about the Ghost Dance. He wired the Indian Bureau time and again for help, asking for at least one thousand troops to rescue him from the Ghost Dancers. A few days after the tense standoff in and around his office, he hightailed it along with his family to Nebraska and stated plainly that he would refuse to return to Pine Ridge without a military escort. His request was granted. When Royer re-entered the reservation, he did so along with one hundred seventy black soldiers representing the Ninth Cavalry, two hundred infantry, a Hotchkiss cannon, and a Gatling gun. Meanwhile, another one hundred ten black cavalrymen and one hundred twenty infantrymen had arrived at Rosebud, the Brule Reservation, as a response to the Ghost Dancing. It marked the first time U.S. soldiers had been dispatched against the Lakota since the late 1870s.

Retreat to Stronghold

The sight of troops motivated many of the Indians, including some one thousand Brule, to flee. Kicking Bear and Short Bull directed them out of the reservations and into an area known as Stronghold, a triangular plateau about three miles long and two miles wide in the Badlands. They planned to survive through the winter on the wild game and livestock they had taken with them. Many donned their Ghost Shirts and performed the Ghost Dance day and night. Short Bull urged them to keep dancing if troops arrived, claiming that if the soldiers attempted to halt the ceremonies, their horses would sink into the earth, as would the men who dismounted from them. The Sioux who didn't believe that were prepared to fight. If the soldiers followed them, six hundred warriors were ready to go to battle just as their brothers had done at Little Bighorn fourteen years earlier.

That was a scenario the government wished desperately to avoid. General Nelson Miles ordered Brigadier General John Brooke, who was the officer in charge of Pine Ridge and Rose-bud, to convince the renegade Indians to surrender. Understand-ing that military intervention could result in a bloodbath, Brooke dispatched seventy-year-old Catholic missionary John Jutz, who was well liked by the Sioux. Jutz spoke with Ghost Dance advocates Short Bull and Kicking Bear, as well as greatly admired and venerable Brule chief Two Strike, a traditionalist and strong opponent of U.S. government policies. Just days ear-lier, Two Strike had threatened to stab General Brooke. Jutz, however, convinced Two Strike and other chiefs to ride into Pine Ridge and meet with Brooke.

Accompanied by Jutz, Two Strike and a number of other chiefs rode back to Pine Ridge, surrounded by twenty-four young war-riors, who were added to the party by the chiefs due to their sus-picion that the scheduled meeting with Brooke was merely a ruse to capture them. The Indians were decorated with war paint and feathers and many had donned their Ghost Dance re-galia. It was in a warlike frame of mind that they met with Brooke, who first offered plenty of food and jobs as scouts if they brought their fellow Sioux close to the reservation, where he could remain in touch with them. Brooke said he hoped the Indi-ans were open to a non-violent solution and that the soldiers had only been summoned to protect the settlers and keep the peace. But the Indians returned to Stronghold having promised nothing.

Miles chastised Brooke for being unable to negotiate surren-der, which forced the latter to send thirty-two Lakota allies and bi-racial scout Louis Shangreau to Stronghold in an effort to bring the holdouts in. They were confronted by Short Bull, who told Shangreau that if the Great Father (president Benjamin Harrison) would allow them to continue performing the Ghost Dance, provide more rations, and end all talk about downsizing the reservation, he would advocate a return. But Short Bull also expressed grave doubts about the sincerity of white leaders, claiming that they had been deceived by Indian agents so often that they didn't know what they could believe.

> "If we return he will take away our guns and ponies, put some of us in jail for stealing cattle and plundering houses (which the Sioux had indeed done in their travels to the Badlands)," Short Bull said. "We prefer to stay here and die, if necessary, to loss of liberty. We are free now and have plenty of beef, can dance all the time in obedience to the command of (the Great Spirit). We tell you to return to your agent and say to him that the Dakotas in the Badlands are not going to come in."[6]

Shangreau wasn't about to leave, a defeated man. He remained at Stronghold for two more days while the Ghost Dance was performed without end. While Shangreau and the Indians prepared to meet on the third day, Two Strike suddenly rose and stunned one and all by announcing his plan to escort his people back to Pine Ridge and surrender. Brule chief Crow Dog followed suit. The shocking news prompted Short Bull to call for his fellow Indians to remain strong and together. He also accused Shangreau of being a traitor and urged his warriors to kill the man. Short Bull's followers indeed held up their rifles like clubs, but the Indians who had accompanied Shangreau on the trip formed a shield around him and Two Strike's men also moved in to protect him. A fight broke out, but Crow Dog quelled it by peacefully placing a blanket over his head and remaining silent. The Indians on both sides of the battle stopped and looked at him, after which Crow Dog reiterated his plan to return to the reservation.

About half the Indians followed him and the rest soon joined them on the way back to Pine Ridge. But as they rode toward the agency, Short Bull and Kicking Bear began to discuss their fate and grew fearful that they would be sent to prison. They convinced a few who still strongly believed in the powers of the

Ghost Dance to accompany them back to the Stronghold. Meanwhile, about nine hundred of Two Strike's Brule continued on to their surrender. Most had come to the conclusion that the Ghost Dancing they had been performing for months had brought neither their dead Indian brothers nor the buffalo back to life, so the practice was of no use.

Despite the small number of holdouts in the Badlands, the Ghost Dance controversy could have met a comparatively peaceful end at that point. But McLaughlin's intense and seemingly unreasonable hatred for Sitting Bull not only prevented a nonviolent conclusion to the chapter in American history, but also led to its most horrific massacre.

McLaughlin was generally applauded for his efforts. Even a representative of the Indian Rights Association lauded his work in 1886, praising him for his assistance in bringing education and farming to the natives. Sitting Bull had indeed been quite set in his ways and was tied to the traditions, customs, and ways of life of the Sioux. But he had also made a concerted effort to assimilate, urging the Indian children to attend school and set a path toward a promising future in the white world. He had even forged a new life as a farmer quite successfully on the reservation. Yet McLaughlin appeared undaunted in his drive to end Sitting Bull's influence.

Arresting the Hunkpapa chief would be no easy task. Sitting Bull was widely accepted and even revered in the white world after he had made millions of friends traveling with Buffalo Bill Cody in the Wild West show. He was arguably the most famous and beloved Indian in all of America. Government officials had repeatedly rejected McLaughlin's requests to have Sitting Bull arrested, but as panic continued to grip the Plains over the Ghost Dance and newspapers fabricated stories about Indian atrocities, Washington finally gave in and ordered that the Sioux leader be taken into custody.

But not only was the popularity of such a move with the American people going to be questioned, but the task itself of arresting Sitting Bull also created problems. Miles offered that the military should perform the deed. McLaughlin believed that was a recipe for a bloody disaster and asserted that the police from nearby Fort Yates should make the arrest. Fort Yates commander Lieutenant Colonel William Drum and his superiors agreed, but Miles hoped to circumvent their authority by dispatching Buffalo Bill Cody to Standing Rock to bring in Sitting Bull. Miles was under the impression that Cody could convince his friend from the Wild West Show days to come in peacefully.

That plan never came to fruition, greatly due to Drum and McLaughlin, who believed that Cody would be killed if he tried to arrest Sitting Bull and the result would be a bloody battle with the Sioux. They escorted Buffalo Bill to the nearest saloon as soon as he arrived at Standing Rock. They plied the notoriously heavy drinker with alcohol, which precluded any possibility that Cody could meet with Sitting Bull that evening. Prepared to ride to Sitting Bull's Grand River compound the next morning, he was given the wrong directions by Drum and McLaughlin and ended up back at the agency. By that time the government had rescinded the order to Cody and placed the responsibility for arresting Sitting Bull on McLaughlin.

One idea failed. Drum had planned to surround Standing Rock with troops on a Saturday when Sitting Bull arrived to receive his rations, but the chief always sent a family member to perform that task. Sitting Bull had been warned by his fellow Indians that he could be arrested if he ever showed up to the agency.

Meanwhile, the Ghost Dancing had virtually ceased at Standing Rock due to various factors, including bitter cold temperatures, exhaustion, and the presence of troops surrounding the reservation. The Indians understood that with only about one hundred warriors they were no match for the number of soldiers available to McLaughlin.

Yet the government remained wary, ordering all white settlers to remain close to the agency, where they could be easily protected from an attack by renegade Sioux. Rumors had again circulated that the Indians had left the reservation and were preparing to go to war. One white who ignored the warning was congregational missionary Mary Collins, who was trusted and loved by the Indians. She decided in early December to travel to Sitting Bull's camp to speak with him. Collins arrived for prayer services on a Sunday and was taken aback by the wild dancing and screaming that accompanied the singing of "Nearer My God to Thee." The Ghost Dancing practiced by Sitting Bull's followers had even infiltrated religious Christian ceremonies. Collins minced no words in telling Sitting Bull what was on her mind.

> "You know you do not believe these things that you are telling your people," she said. "You know that the Indians have not risen from the death out in the White Mountains and that the buffalo and deer and your favorite hunting dogs are not alive again. You know that you are deceiving your people who have always trusted you. The law orders you to go to Fort Yates and you must obey. You must go and talk with the officials there and tell them that you will have this dance cease. Otherwise the soldiers will come and kill all of your people. Your best warriors and men will be shot and the families will go unprovided for, and you, Sitting Bull, will be responsible for this terrible calamity. You must send the people home."[7]

Collins claimed that Sitting Bull replied that the Ghost Dance religion had already gone too far and that he couldn't put a halt to it because his people would laugh at him. She urged him to tell his followers to stop dancing, but to no avail. But he did ask her to deliver the message, which she proceeded to do. She emerged from Sitting Bull's tent and gazed her eyes upon hundreds of Indians dancing wildly. One she knew well as Louie dropped to the ground and Collins believed him to be feigning unconsciousness. She sidled up next to him and lectured him, saying that she knew he was pretending and that he should tell his fellow dancers to go home. Collins added that when Louie rose to his feet, the Indians lost faith in the Ghost Dance because they had seen the fakery.

Despite this incident, Collins stated her view to McLaughlin that Sitting Bull was no danger to anyone. And though McLaughlin concurred, he still sought permission to have him arrested. He believed reports that Sitting Bull was planning on leaving Standing Rock and joining his Sioux brothers who remained free at Stronghold. But it seemed McLaughlin believed what he wanted to believe. Sitting Bull had forty-five head of cattle, plenty of hay, and a field of oats cut and was going nowhere.

McLaughlin, however, accepted the word of informants who claimed that the Hunkpapa leader was heading to the Badlands. And Miles agreed, ordering Colonel Drum to make arrange-ments to have Sitting Bull arrested. Much to Miles' dismay, Drum turned the job over to McLaughlin, who selected for the task a "friendly" Sioux named Bull Head. Despite his hatred for Sitting Bull that stemmed from a fight during a buffalo hunt years earlier, the lieutenant of the Indian police was well respected among his fellow Sioux.

According to One Bull, his friend Sitting Bull had experienced a vision in the fall of 1890 in which he saw himself being killed by his own tribesmen. That vision was soon to become reality.

Notes

1. McLaughlin, James. *My Friend the Indian*. Boston and New York: Houghton Mifflin, 1910. 185–87 [accessed October 2009]. http://books .google.com/books?id=YgYcAAAAMAAJ&dq=james+mclaughlin: +my+friend+the+india&printsec=frontcover&source=bl&ots=m_5 RYEOfsJ&sig=FL3OndZDRlyTnP3RRew4SRW988Q&hl=en&ei=jSOf SrTjO5PMMrnqwKoK&sa=X&oi=book_result&ct=result&resnum= 5#v=onepage&q=&f=false

2. Ibid. 15.

3. Jenson, Richard E., Paul, Eli R. and Carter, John E. *Eyewitness at Wounded Knee*. Lincoln, NB: University of Nebraska Press. 6.

4. McLaughlin, James. *My Friend the Indian*. Boston and New York: Houghton Mifflin, 1910. 202–04 [accessed October 2009]. http://books .google.com/books?id=YgYcAAAAMAAJ&dq=james+mclaughlin: +my+friend+the+india&printsec=frontcover&source=bl&ots=m_5 RYEOfsJ&sig=FL3OndZDRlyTnP3RRew4SRW988Q&hl=en&ei=jSOf SrTjO5PMMrnqwKoK&sa=X&oi=book_result&ct=result&resnum= 5#v=onepage&q=&f=false

5. Eastman, Charles. *From the Deep Woods to Civilization*. Boston: Little, Brown and Company, 1916. 1080–9. Reprinted by Dover Publications, 2003.

6. Utley, Robert M. *The Last Days of the Sioux Nation*. New Haven, CT: Yale University Press, 1963. 118.

7. Coleman, William S.E. *Voices of Wounded Knee*. Lincoln, NB: Uni-versity of Nebraska Press, 2000. 178.

FIVE

Prelude to a Slaughter

THOUGH DRUM TURNED THE job of arresting Sitting Bull to McLaughlin's Indian police, led by Bull Head, the major wouldn't be idle in the proceedings. His troops would arrive to lend support after the deed was done. That would not only place the blame for any problems on McLaughlin, but it would also prevent the army from incurring any casualties, which was most likely to occur at the time of the arrest.

On the frigid, snowy night of December 14, the Indian police gathered at Bull Head's house, which rested on Grand River just a few miles from Sitting Bull's camp. Converts to Christianity, they prayed to the white man's god, yet felt more than a twinge of regret about the task that had been laid in front of them. They arrived at dawn while the Indians were asleep and barged into Sitting Bull's home. The Hunkpapa chief had long lost his militancy and was expecting such an intrusion eventually, so he agreed to be escorted away peacefully.

But there would be no peace. Sitting Bull's now awakened followers gathered, including his fourteen-year-old son, Crow Foot, who chastised his father for giving in so meekly. Hearing such defiant words from his child prompted Sitting Bull to change his mind and refuse to go. Bull Head and Lone Man urged Sitting Bull to ignore the advice, but to no avail. Soon Sitting Bull's Sioux began to taunt and threaten the Indian police. Others arrived with guns, which prompted Bull Head to call for calm. His words were in vain. Followers of Sitting Bull began moving closer to protect him while insisting that they would not allow their chief to be arrested. Though they had yet to attack the

71

police, commotion was overtaking calm. A horse on which Sitting Bull was supposed to ride was saddled, but he cried out that he would be killed before he succumbed. The police, who had now surrounded him, informed him that soldiers were nearby, but that there would be no trouble if he came with them peacefully.

Sitting Bull finally relented and agreed to go, but fellow tribesman Catch-the-Bear and others broke through the police cordon. One urged that the old police should be killed first because the young ones would then flee. Suddenly shots rang out, prompting Drum and his men to ride into the camp and begin firing at Sitting Bull's people, scattering them in the process. But when the smoke from the guns had cleared, the unarmed Sitting Bull and Crow Foot were dead and Bull Head had been fatally wounded. Accounts vary as to who killed Sitting Bull. Lone Man and Shoots Walking claimed it was Bull Head, though the former asserts that an Indian policeman named Red Tomahawk fired the bullet that finished Sitting Bull off. Gray Eagle, however, stated that Red Tomahawk killed Sitting Bull after Bull Head had been hit.

The brutality continued even after the shooting was over, particularly against the dead Hunkpapa leader. He was cut across the face with an ax and struck in the head with a club. One of the officers finally assigned a man to guard his body after yet another had struck him with a riding whip.

The killing of Sitting Bull prompted a myriad of responses and emotions throughout the nation. Many Americans agreed with Indian rights advocates that white greed and an agent in McLaughlin who felt unjustifiably threatened by Sitting Bull used the Ghost Dancing as an excuse to convince the government to have him arrested, which ultimately resulted in the chief's demise. Others, however, believed in the perceived righteousness of Manifest Destiny, which asserted the inevitability of the white man taking over the continent and the red man being destroyed. Among those who held neither view but shed no tears over the death of Sitting Bull was newspaper editor L. Frank Baum, who later penned the classic children's book, *The Wonderful Wizard of Oz*. On December 20, 1890, Baum offered his opinions in the *Aberdeen Saturday Pioneer*.

"(Sitting Bull) was an Indian with a white man's spirit of hatred and revenge for those who had wronged him and his," Baum wrote. "In his day he saw his son and his tribe gradually driven from their possessions; forced to give up their hunting grounds and espouse the hard working and uncongenial avocations of the whites. And these, his conquerors, were marked in their dealings with his people by selfishness, falsehood and treachery. What wonder that his wild nature, untamed by years of subjection, should still revolt? What wonder that a fiery rage still burned within his breast and that he should seek every opportunity of obtaining vengeance upon his natural enemies?

"The proud spirit of the original owners of these vast prairies inherited through centuries of fierce and bloody wars for their possession, lingered last in the bosom of Sitting Bull. With his fall the nobility of the Redskin is exterminated and what few are left are a pack of whining curs who lick the hand that smites them. The Whites, by law of conquest, by justice and civilization, are masters of the American continent, and the best safety of the frontier settlements will be secured by the total annihilation of the few remaining Indians. Why annihilation? Their glory has fled, their spirit broken, their manhood effaced; better that they die than live the miserable wretches that they are. History would forget these latter despicable beings, and speak, in later ages of the glory of these grand Kings of the forest and plain. . . ."[1]

The followers of Sitting Bull who survived the gun battle panicked and fled either to join Big Foot, whose small band was still roaming free along the Little Missouri River, or the still practicing Ghost Dancers at Stronghold. In a letter to the Indian Commissioner in Washington, McLaughlin claimed wrongly that the Indian police had been surrounded in the battle. He also contended that about one hundred Hunkpapa men had deserted their families and fled. Actually, the figure was closer to seventy-five and many of them had surrendered during the course of the battle. Fewer than forty men, women, and children joined Big Foot and merely a dozen were of fighting age. Yet newspaper reporters from around the area, who also greatly exaggerated the number of Indians roaming the Badlands, claimed that they were preparing to attack.

The army knew otherwise. Hardened former Indian fighter Brigadier General Wesley Merritt told reporters in late December that the death of Sitting Bull marked the end of any threat of armed insurrection. He added that he had even deemed it improbable before the chief had been killed, citing the coming of winter and the necessities for the Indians of food and shelter, as well as the fact that they were poorly armed. Merritt scoffed at the notion that Indians no matter how naïve could possibly still believe in heavenly intervention. And he added that though the Sioux did boast some Winchester repeating rifles, they didn't own enough horses to maximize their fighting potential. Merritt also stated in a thinly veiled jab at Miles that there were some in the military who continued to issue orders dispatching troops to Indian reservations to further their own personal ambitions. Merritt expressed his belief that the end of Sitting Bull's influence would mean the end of trouble with the Sioux.

Mourning Sitting Bull's Death

Meanwhile, the Sioux—"hostiles" and Indian police alike—were exhibiting great sorrow. The wives and children of the dead wept, cried, and sang about their grief. Newspapers reported that some of the women slashed off pieces of their fingers and other parts of their bodies, as was a tribe custom. The Indian police who survived felt sick about killing their own brothers. Among those killed was Shave Head, who in his death throes told doctors and agency officials that he would perish in the faith of the white man and was proud that his children were following in that same path.

Sitting Bull received no respect from the agency even in death. His body was placed in a dump cart and tossed into a hole in the ground of the military cemetery without a gravestone. He was buried in that spot because the surviving family members of the Indian police objected to having him buried among their dead. But Sitting Bull's body was eventually removed by his relatives and buried around his birthplace in the Grand River Valley.

American politicians were split on the justification of Sitting Bull's murder. On December 22, U.S. representative Arthur Bailly-Blanchard of Louisiana offered a resolution to the House that called for an investigation into the killing. Fellow representative

William McAdoo of New Jersey concurred that action should be taken, but nothing was done.

A week earlier, while the carnage was taking place at Standing Rock, General Brooke was planning to advance on the Stronghold, where the militant Short Bull and Kicking Bear were still considered threats, as was the continued Ghost Dancing. But the military measures in the Badlands were delayed because authorities believed the death of Sitting Bull would make it difficult to persuade the friendly Indians to take action against their brothers.

The situation was certainly muddled. At that point, hundreds of Sioux who had left the Stronghold, led by Two Strike, were just miles from Pine Ridge and the venerable Red Cloud was attempting to convince those who remained there to come in as well. But the Hunkpapa and others who fled Standing Rock were headed either to the Stronghold or to Pine Ridge. Settlers throughout the area were sounding the alarm, circulating unfounded rumors that the Sioux were preparing to go to war and fleeing to the cities in fear. And the tragic news of the slaughter at Standing Rock was surely dampening the Christmas spirit of both whites and recently converted Indians.

Yet there was in reality little to worry about. Of the Sioux who survived the shootout at Sitting Bull's Grand River camp, one hundred sixty surrendered immediately. According to army figures, thirty-eight headed for the Little Missouri River, where Big Foot and about three hundred fifty of his Miniconjou were still roaming free. Of those, only fourteen were men of fighting age. Another three hundred loyal Ghost Dancers remained at the Stronghold and McLaughlin reported that about fifty others were headed elsewhere. About seven hundred Indians were off their reservations as the winter of 1890 began. Perhaps one-third of them could be considered warriors. They were hardly a threat, particularly considering that General Miles had gathered more than eight thousand troops in the Dakotas who were preparing to set up camp in the Northern Badlands. The five hundred Lakota lured in as scouts even outnumbered those at the Stronghold.

Miles, however, hoped to avoid violence. He knew that nearby Pine Ridge was being overwhelmed by hundreds of Sioux who had surrendered to authorities. The last thing he wanted to do was turn them violent by slaughtering their helpless Indian brothers at the Stronghold. Miles decided to wait until the Ghost Dancers ran out of food and were forced to come in. He dispatched patrols to prevent them from leaving the area. Miles' soldiers were soon joined by cavalry units commanded by Major Guy V. Henry and Colonel James Forsyth. But their troops were itching for action, at least partly due to their fear of a breakout by enough Sioux to mount an attack. Others, representing the Seventh Cavalry, yearned to avenge the killing of General Custer and his men at the Battle of the Little Bighorn fourteen years earlier.

Meanwhile, the travels of Miniconjou chiefs Big Foot and Hump and their followers were about to end. Big Foot feared that the killing of Sitting Bull signaled the beginning of a white war against the Lakotas and decided to turn himself into Pine Ridge, greatly because of repeated invitations from Red Cloud. Chief Hump, who had been traveling with Big Foot, was also considering surrendering at that agency. Little did they know that Miles, who believed Big Foot was cast from the same mold as Sitting Bull, had ordered Lieutenant Colonel Edwin Sumner to find the Miniconjou chief and arrest him. Big Foot indeed was a traditional Sioux who had embraced the Ghost Dance as possible salvation, but he was not as defiant as Sitting Bull and certainly less of a threat. Miles called for Big Foot and his followers to be brought into the Cheyenne River Reservation and closely watched.

Big Foot had other ideas. Sumner indeed caught up with him, but the cavalry leader proved to be far more sympathetic to the Indian cause than Miles would have liked. Though he informed Big Foot of the illegality of harboring the fugitives of Sitting Bull's band and there was great tension between his soldiers and the Miniconjou, Sumner allowed the chief to lead his tribe into Cheyenne River without army accompaniment. That gave Big Foot the opportunity to slip away from Sumner and his men and accept Red Cloud's invitation to join the Oglala at Pine Ridge.

Eluding Sumner wasn't easy. The cavalry followed the Indians' every move, always camping nearby. When Big Foot asked Sumner why the Miniconjou were being shadowed, the lieutenant colonel replied that his job was to stop the Ghost Dancing, which was still being performed. After a few more days of hide and seek, an army officer arrived at the Miniconjou camp and ordered Big Foot's surrender. Big Foot asked for food for his tribe and a day to think about it. He promised not to attempt an escape, but the soldiers provided no food for his people. And the following morning, the Indians awoke to find that the cavalry remained close by and had aimed a Hotchkiss rapid-firing cannon at their tents.

A Ruse by the Miniconjou

That's when Big Foot agreed to allow the soldiers to take him and his fellow Miniconjou in, but the chief had a bit of trickery in mind. As he rode his pony near the front of the group, he quietly told one of his braves to prepare himself and the others. The young Indian passed the word to the rest of the band—they were going to try to escape. The squaws began tossing everything heavy off their horses, scattering goods everywhere. Big Foot explained to a curious soldier that their ponies were weak and that they needed to lighten the load. He added that the horses needed rest and that they had to camp at that spot, which boasted a favorable water supply.

After the sun descended from the sky, the Indians built fires in a ruse to make the soldiers, who were camping quite a distance away, believe they were indeed settling in for the night. Meanwhile, Big Foot had instructed the braves to put blankets over their shoulders so they would look like squaws from far away while the squaws were riding away in the wagons. When one cavalry messenger boy arrived to ask where the wagons had gone, Big Foot rose to his feet and told his "cross-dressing" braves to help show the soldier where the wagons were. Stunned to see that there were braves underneath the blankets, the overreacting messenger raced away screaming that the soldiers were under attack. Big Foot and his Miniconjou then hopped on their horses and sped off, eventually catching up to their squaws. They all rode like the wind throughout the night and were in the Badlands the next day. More than 350 Miniconjou had escaped from Sumner and his cavalry unit—and General Miles was livid.

News from Stronghold did nothing to improve his mood. Fifty Pine Ridge Sioux agency officials deemed as friendly Indians were dispatched to Short Bull's camp to persuade him and his Brule to come in. That merely angered the Stronghold holdouts, who shot their guns over the heads of the agency Indians and told them in no uncertain terms to leave, which they did. Five days later one hundred fifty Pine Ridge Indians returned, only to receive the same treatment. Undaunted, a group of prominent Brule and Oglala chiefs met with General Brooke on December 20 and asked if they could be sent out to convince the hostiles to surrender. The frustrated Brooke consented and about two hundred Indians set out for the Stronghold two days later. The contingent included a small but strong band of warriors who were prepared to take violent action if the request to Short Bull's men to surrender was again refused.

The third time was the charm. The following morning, Short Bull sent everyone to Pine Ridge but him and his uncle, who followed them that night. The Brule chief wanted to enjoy a few extra days of freedom, particularly since he was fearful that he would be placed under arrest upon his arrival at the agency. He figured that it would be best to surrender after those who had spent months with him at the Stronghold had come in.

Big Foot too wished to be free, but he was becoming quite sick with pneumonia. Three from his band were sent to Pine Ridge to deliver the message that Big Foot was ill and on the way in. The following morning three Pine Ridge Indians came out to inform Big Foot that since Short Bull's entire camp was arriving in two days, they would like him to do the same. Furthermore, they warned Big Foot that soldiers were at nearby Wounded Knee Creek. They suggested that he avoid them on the way.

While Big Foot was beginning his trek, Brooke was dispatching troops from the Sixth, Seventh, Eighth, and Ninth Cavalry regiments to begin a wide and intensified search in freezing weather to find Big Foot's band and make certain it didn't reach the Badlands. Heading the charge were Seventh Cavalry troops under Colonel Forsyth and commanded by the seasoned Major Samuel Whitside. That unit headed out to Wounded Knee Creek in an attempt to intercept the ailing Big Foot. When they arrived at Wounded Knee the day after Christmas, the Indians were moving slowly toward their Pine Ridge destination due to their chief's illness. By December 27, he decided he could no longer travel and urged his people to leave him at Medicine Root Creek. The Miniconjou remained there for two days, after which Big Foot said that he wanted to reach Red Cloud's camp at Pine Ridge before he died. By that time, however, Miles had become impatient and had ordered Brooke to take steps to have all the free Indians rounded up, disarmed, and guarded closely. Brooke replied that the task would be done, adding that the Indians who deceived and escaped from Sumner would not get away this time.

Whitside and his Seventh Cavalry confronted Big Foot's band west of Porcupine Creek and ordered the chief to surrender immediately. Big Foot extended his hand and told the major that he was sick and that his people wanted peace, but Whitside interrupted him, informing the Miniconjou leader that his two choices were to fight or to surrender. The latter was quickly accepted. Whitside asked Big Foot to turn in twenty-five guns, to which Big Foot answered that if he did so, he feared the soldiers would use them to harm his people, so he preferred to wait until they arrived at the agency. Whitside let it slide, offering his view that those who claimed that Big Foot was hostile were lying. He even called for an ambulance to transport the sick chief.

The veteran major then wrote his superiors announcing the capture of one hundred twenty men and two hundred fifty women and children and requested that the second battalion of the Seventh Cavalry, led by Colonel James Forsyth, be dispatched as reinforcements to assume the task of disarming the Indians. The five-mile march toward Wounded Knee Creek, where those tasks were to be done, then began, led by the ambulance holding Big Foot and the troops and followed by about forty Sioux on horseback. The Ghost Dancers coming in to Pine Ridge from the Stronghold were camping only five miles away from the agency, so it appeared that any threat of Indian violence had subsided.

Whitside's men and the Lakota arrived at Wounded Knee late in the afternoon of December 28. The soldiers transported Big

Foot from the ambulance into an army tent and provided dinner to the Indians. But the surrendering of arms became a bone of contention. Some inferior weapons were turned in, which the Miniconjou claimed was all they had in their possession. White civilians on the scene concurred, stating that indeed the Indians were poorly armed. The army, however, suspected that they were carrying concealed weapons. While Whitside awaited Forsythe and the Seventh Cavalry, he strengthened the hold on his captives, setting up rapid-fire Hotchkiss guns to overlook the camp. He also dispatched a courier to summon General Brooke from the Pine Ridge Agency to join the Second Battalion of the Seventh Cavalry. The idea was that through military intimidation and sheer numbers, the Indians would be easily convinced to disarm without incident.

Prelude to a Massacre

Those sheer numbers continued to pile up that night upon the arrival of Forsyth and his Second Battalion. According to Whitside, the colonel took great precaution to keep his presence and that of his men secret from the Indians, but that is unlikely considering the fact that he brought with him three hundred armed and mounted soldiers, as well as wagons and artillery into a rather narrow passageway. But a subsequent letter from Forsyth to Pine Ridge confirmed his intention to join Whitside in bringing the Indians back to the agency once they had been disarmed the following morning. By that evening the number of trained soldiers at Wounded Knee had reached five hundred. Those of fighting age representing Big Foot's tribe totaled barely more than one hundred, most of which were not mounted.

The Indians hoped to settle in for the night without incident, but the behavior of the soldiers precluded that from happening. They tried to stay warm in their tipis along the banks of the creek. The second battalion soldiers of Troop E positioned themselves on a western hill, which allowed them to peer easily into the Miniconjou camp. They aimed four Hotchkiss guns at the Indians, who could consider neither escape nor attack. All seemed secure. Word had even reached Pine Ridge that many from the Badlands bands of Short Bull and Kicking Bear were just a few hours away from the agency.

The situation was also attracting media attention. The impending surrender of a dying Big Foot brought a number of reporters to Wounded Knee. Others streamed into Pine Ridge to witness the surrender of Short Bull and the Ghost Dancers. A number of other thrill-seeking civilians joined them in anticipation of watching the event. Little could any of them have predicted the violence that would eventually follow, though later investigations revealed that the soldiers on the night of December 28 were getting quite drunk on whisky that had been smuggled in from traders. A freighter named Swigert later admitted that he felt more than a twinge of guilt throughout his life for having delivered the booze to the men who would the following morning embark on the most horrific mass slaughter in U.S. history.

> "It was too bad those drunken soldiers were allowed to handle a delicate situation," Swigert said. "I know they were all drunk. I am sorry because I feel partly responsible in hauling whiskey in with the supplies. If it was not for this liquor, I don't believe the massacre of the natives by the white soldiers would have occurred."[2]

According to some witnesses, the imbibing soldiers didn't get much sleep. Some staggered over to Forsyth's tent to congratulate him on capturing the Miniconjou. Others attempted to remove the dying Big Foot from his temp, but were stopped. Meanwhile, whisky was being passed from tent to tent. The activity prevented the Indians from sleeping soundly.

So did occasional questioning from soldiers, some of whom had played a role in the Battle of the Little Bighorn in 1876 and still bore grudges. Some from the latest incarnation of the Seventh Cavalry attempted to identify Indians who had fought in the legendary battle in which General Custer and the same cavalry group of the past generation had been destroyed. Nineteen of the men representing the Seventh Cavalry at Wounded Knee—including seven officers—had been there. Though any intention of the soldiers to exact revenge for the events at Bighorn has never been proven, one minister at Pine Ridge claimed he both overheard and spoke directly with soldiers who were eagerly anticipating an opportunity to do just that.

Before sunrise, Chief Horn Cloud gathered his sons together and warned them that he expected fighting that day. Miniconjou survivor Dewey Beard remembered his father saying,

"I have been in war all my life, and I know when my heart is growing bitter that there is going to be a fight, and I have come to tell you—all my sons, what I want you to do. If one or two Indians go to start trouble, I don't want you to go with them. Don't you join them.

"Besides this, if the white people start trouble first, then you can do what you want to—you can die among your own relations in defending them. All you, my dear sons, stand together and keep yourselves sober, and all of you, if you die at once among your relations defending them, I will be satisfied. Try to die in front of your relations, the old folks and the little ones, and I will be satisfied if you die trying to help them. Don't get excited.

"When one or two under the government laws start trouble they are arrested and taken into court and put in jail, but I don't want any of you to get into such trouble, but to stand back until all the whites assail us, and then defend our people. I have come to tell you this as advice before the trouble begins. I want you to heed my warnings."[3]

A bugle sounded at dawn and the Indians awoke to find the camp buzzing with activity. Breakfast was eaten quickly while the Lakota were loading up their wagons for the excursion to Pine Ridge. Despite the ominous signals sent the previous evening, the warning of violence from Horn Cloud wasn't accompanied by an atmosphere of fear. The Miniconjou children played near their tipis, which led the soldiers to believe that all was well and that the Indians were certainly planning no revolt. A group that had congregated in Big Foot's tent for a council was informed by an Indian scout that as soon as it had ended, the trek to the agency would begin.

At least that's what the Indians were led to believe. By that time, Whitside and Forsyth had been informed of General Brooke's real intentions: To ship Big Foot and his Miniconjou to the Union Pacific Railroad in Gordon, Nebraska, for a trip to a military prison in Omaha. Brooke had told Miles of his plan upon Big Foot's capture, but Forsyth wasn't clued in until various dispatches were received from Pine Ridge. He, in turn, told Whitside about the orders. Among the communications was one addressed to Whitside that a courier delivered early on the fateful morning of December 29. It read:

"The Condg Genrl. directs that you proceed with your Battalion and the Indian prisoners to Gordon, Neb., where you will transfer the Indians to Colonel Frank Wheaton, 2d Infantry, on Dec. 30th, if possible. The ponies and wagons will not accompany the Indians further from Gordon, and you will bring them with you on your return to this [Pine Ridge], which will begin as soon as you transfer the Indians to Colonel Wheaton."[4]

The deception was to continue until the last moment, but as it turned out, the Miniconjou wouldn't live to gain awareness of the plan to dispatch them to Omaha. Their squaws packed for the trip to Pine Ridge while the men held their council, though a few days later some of Forsyth's officers stated that the Miniconjou were preparing to flee. That claim loses merit when considering that the Indians were surrounded by soldiers.

Before they all were to depart, Forsyth demanded that the Indians disarm. According to Lakota interpreter John Shangrau, some of the Indians complained that they were told they could keep their guns until they arrived at Pine Ridge, but added that they were willing to negotiate. Speaking to one another, the Indians decided to visit Big Foot, whose word would be final. Shangrau stated that he followed two Indians into the tent to see the dying chief, who told them to give up some of the bad guns but keep the good ones. Shangrau intervened, asking the Indians to give up all their guns. After all, he said, they could always acquire new ones, but they couldn't bring dead Indians back to life. Big Foot, however, was adamant. He insisted that the Indians surrender only their inferior weapons.

The Miniconjou began stacking up their arms and guns in the center of the camp. That was, of course, unsatisfactory to Forsyth, who ordered that they bring in more weapons. Big Foot, who was coughing and had blood running from his nose, saw no other options and requested that his warriors comply. About twenty-five additional guns were surrendered, but the army leaders remained suspicious that the Indians were still hiding weapons, so General George Wallace was dispatched to accompany several of his men into the tipis to search for more. They began bringing out and stacking anything that could be used in an attack, including axes, bows and arrows, knives, and tent stakes. The soldiers then ordered the Indians to remove their blankets for a further search. An angry Miniconjou medicine man named Yellow Bird reacted by taking a few Ghost Dance steps and chanting to his fellow tribesmen that the soldiers' bullets could not penetrate their sacred clothing, but the others complied.

By that time, nearly all the weapons had been confiscated, but Forsyth believed there to be more. He instructed scout and translator Philip Wells to tell the Indians that after all the guns and knives were surrendered, they were to line up along the edge of the water while soldiers held unloaded guns to their foreheads. This rather nonsensical act, which again leads to speculation that the effects of the whisky from the night before hadn't fully subsided by the morning, would be punishment to the Indians who did not turn in their weapons when asked.

> "My legs were trembling and my heart was thumping and I was afraid," Dewey Beard said. "We did not understand the soldier's orders. We could not comprehend this foolishness. But this offended and angered us, and we reasoned among ourselves and said we were human beings and not cattle to be used this way. We are people in this world.
>
> "Most of us had given up our arms; there were a few standing with their guns, but the soldiers had not been to them. The knives were piled up in the center of the council; some young men had their guns and knives, but they had not been asked for them."[5]

Forsyth became flustered and impatient by Yellow Bird's continued incantations. It was upon the completion of the medicine man's Ghost Dance that tension turned into tragedy. The soldiers were busily loading their weapons. Some were holding them in fire position. Trading store owner Louis Mousseau later stated that a total of sixty-nine guns had been placed in two piles, leading to estimates that no more than five weapons remained in the possession of the Indians by the time the massacre began.

At that point the soldier search party came upon two young Indians who still held Winchesters. One of them belonged to a young, deaf Miniconjou and nephew of Big Foot named Black Coyote, who raised it over his head and shouted that he had spent a great deal of money for it and he wasn't about to give it up. Dewey Beard later claimed that Black Coyote would have eventually succumbed and turned it in if left alone, but soldiers grabbed the deaf Indian and spun him around while violently trying to yank the gun from his hands. The Wounded Knee Massacre was moments away.

Notes

1. Venable, Robert. "Looking Back at Wounded Knee 1890," *Northeast Indian Quarterly*, Spring 1990. Twisted Footnote to Wounded Knee [accessed November 2009]. http://www.dickshovel.com/TwistedFootnote.html

2. Coleman, William S.E. *Voices of Wounded Knee*. Lincoln, Nebraska: University of Nebraska Press, 2000. 273.

3. Danker, Donald F. "The Wounded Knee Interviews of Eli S. Ricker," *Nebraska History* (1981): 190.

4. Coleman, William S.E. *Voices of Wounded Knee*. Lincoln, Nebraska: University of Nebraska Press, 2000. 280–81.

5. Danker, Donald F., "The Wounded Knee Interviews of Eli S. Ricker," *Nebraska History* (1981): 191.

SIX

The Massacre and Its Aftermath

CONSIDERING THE NUMBER OF cavalry men, Indian survivors and civilians at Wounded Knee, one might believe there is a definitive account of the tragedy. But it seems that for every person who bore witness to the event, a different story is told.

One of several discrepancies revolves around whether the Indians remained well armed. Soldiers have stated that indeed the Miniconjou still had plenty of weapons that had not been confiscated. Others, including Dewey Beard, have contradicted that view, stating that the Winchester Black Coyote fought to keep was one of the only weapons in their possession.

That disagreement leads to others, such as whether the soldiers were under attack. One side claims that indeed the Indians began firing their guns and perhaps even picked up more weapons off the pile to use against the cavalry men. Those who recall otherwise describe what happened as an indiscriminate and unprovoked slaughter.

What seems certain is that in the struggle with Black Coyote, his gun discharged. Whitside claimed that the gunshot prompted the Indians to throw off their blankets and begin shooting at the troops. Captain Charles A. Varnum added that his troops were even knifed by the Miniconjou. But neither officer explained how the Indians could have armed themselves so quickly when all their weapons had been confiscated, particularly if they had to rush over to the stack of guns and begin shooting. What is more likely is that the gunfire was coming from troops on the opposite side of the circle.

Miniconjou, Paul High Back conceded that there were two Indians who indeed had guns, but contended that neither raised them to fire. He stated that the soldiers simply began shooting at the Indian men, women, and children. Scout and translator Philip Wells concurred, recalling that Forsyth gave the order to fire. Lieutenant James D. Mann claimed it was not Forsyth, but he who issued the order, adding that his men were provoked.

> "In front of me were four bucks—three armed with rifles and one with bow and arrows," Mann stated on his deathbed a few days later. "I drew my revolver and stepped through the line to my place with my detachment. The Indians raised their weapons over their heads as if in votive offering, then brought them down to bear on us, the one with the bow and arrow aiming directly at me. They seemed to wait an instant. The medicine man threw a handful of dust into the air, put on his war bonnet, and then I heard a gun fired near him. This seemed to be the signal they were waiting for, and the fire immediately began."[1]

It was then, according to Mann, that he ordered his men to shoot back.

Whitside claimed that at least fifty shots were fired by the Indians before the soldiers returned the volleys, but that contention seems far-fetched considering the lack of arms available to the Miniconjou. Mousseau offered that many of the Indians were killed before they could reach the stack of guns. He said by that time smoke filled the air. For a short period, small groups of Indians and soldiers grappled in hand-to-hand combat with knives, clubs, and pistols. But according to High Back, the Miniconjou never had an opportunity to return fire.

"We had no chance to fight back as we had no weapons," High Back said. "All we thought about, those of us who were still alive, was to get away. The morning was cloudy and damp and the smoke from the guns did not rise but settled right on us. From then on nothing could be seen very plain. The soldiers were rushing around shooting all of us they could see to shoot."[2] High Back added that many Indians took refuge in a gully to the south of the shooting, but were also gunned down, and that he survived only by crawling under the dead bodies. He stated, however, that he was shot in the hand, forearm, and leg.

Soon the soldiers opened fire from the hill with the Hotchkiss guns, which shot at the rate of nearly one shell a second. They raked the fleeing Indian men, women, and children with shrapnel.

One Indian survivor, Louise Weasel Bear, bitterly condemned the soldiers for killing women and children, claiming that Indian warriors were taught not to fire at white women and children.

Richard Stirk, the white store owner who bore witness to the event, offered that most of the Miniconjou lay dead less than ten minutes after the first gunshot. According to Lieutenant Alexander Piper, many of the casualties suffered by cavalry men were the result of friendly fire. Forsyth had either ignored or forgotten orders from Miles to keep his men separated from the Indians at all times. The result was chaotic.

Among those lay dying was Big Foot. According to reporter Charles Allen, who was on sight, Big Foot's daughter ran toward her father, who was shot just before she arrived. She let out a cry and stooped over him. At that point an officer seized a gun from a fellow soldier and killed her execution-style. Other accounts, however, claim that Big Foot was killed in the initial shooting.

Hunting Down the Fleeing Indians

Indian survivors weren't the only people describing the event as a slaughter and claiming that, even after the initial volleys killed most of the Miniconjou, the soldiers continued to track down and murder even the youngest and most helpless Indians. Anthropologist Warren K. Moorehead recalled watching a twelve-year-old boy in flight being pursued and shot by a soldier. Seventh Cavalry assistant surgeon Frank J. Ives reported gunshot wounds to Indian children ages one and five. A *Rapid City* (South Dakota) *Daily Journal* correspondent wrote the following:

"One little boy nine or ten years old told a pitiful story as he lay wounded in the hospital. He was in Big Foot's camp when the fight commenced and hand in hand with another little fellow of about the same age; he started out at the head of the gully so often referred to as the scene of the greatest carnage. They ran to the top of the hill, when a soldier came in pursuit riding a white horse. When the trooper rode nearly up to them he dismounted, dropped to one knee and shot the narrator's companion through the head. 'He then,' continued the little sufferer, 'fired again, the ball striking me in the leg. I fell and the soldier got on his horse and rode away.'"³

Moorehead offered his view that it was inexcusable that twenty-six children under the age of thirteen were killed at Wounded Knee. Included were four babies found with crushed skulls, most likely the victims of a blow to the head with a butt of a musket or heavy club. Despite such evidence from Ives and Moorehead, cavalry commander H. J. Nowlan claimed that the women and children were spared. Yet *Nebraska State Journal* reporter William Fitch Kelley stated that the troops dismounted to chase down and kill fleeing Indians, including women and children entering the ravine. It was believed by many that some from the Seventh Cavalry were filled with feelings of revenge for its defeat at Little Bighorn.

Even First Sergeant Ragmar Theodor Ling-Vannerus, who claimed that he and his fellow cavalry men took heavy fire from the Indians at the start of the battle, admitted that it deteriorated into a massacre. Ling-Vannerus described events after the Hotchkiss guns began firing and the surviving Indians fled:

> "When the shelling started, all red women and children in the camp had immediately taken to flight. Unrestrainably, they threw themselves into carts or rushed desperately away—some up the valley to the right, others again in wild panic towards the ravine down whose sides they blindly rode, drove, or precipitated themselves, only to be massacred against the rugged rocks at the bottom or to be shot down without mercy by the skirmish line on the opposite side. Here we found them now, in big heaps, piled on each other. Women, the children in their arms, young and old, horses and mules in various positions, broken carts and clothing. More scattered, the warriors lay on their faces, still clutching their weapons.
>
> "There lies a whole family, except the father, under an overturned cart body, with the horses still in the shafts, with their legs crushed, they are writhing in agony. There a papoose cries by its mother's breast which, cold and insensible, can nourish no more; there lies a young girl with her long hair sticky of blood, hiding her mutilated face—they are all lying there in death's unspeakable majesty. And here rests the beautiful squaw whom yesterday I offered a cigarette—dying, with both her

legs shot off. She lies there without wailing and greets me with a faint smile on her pale lips."[4]

Not all of the Indians in the ravine were helpless. Though Pursued was dying and fellow Miniconjou Dewey Beard and White Lance were injured, they secured three belts of cartridges from soldiers and used them from a ditch that gave them a strong vantage point. Pursued told the other two in his death throes to kill as many soldiers as possible, whereupon Dewey Beard and White Lance fired their guns. The soldiers turned the fast-firing Hotchkiss on them, strafing the ground in front of them. But a Miniconjou named Jim Mesteth estimated that White Lance alone killed twelve soldiers that day.

Though indeed twenty-five soldiers lost their lives at Wounded Knee and another thirty-nine were injured, some were done in by friendly fire. Estimates of the number of Indian dead vary. The initial count of one hundred fifty-three didn't include those who crawled away and died later. The number of Indian deaths has been gauged as high as three hundred, leaving the total of survivors at about fifty, many of whom were finally taken to Pine Ridge.

Some Indians who were healthy enough to escape fled over the ridges, though one group of soldiers pursued them and several were killed a few miles away at White Creek. Other Indians had been hit by gunfire and lay wounded. Meanwhile, word of the massacre had reached the agency eighteen miles away, though initial reports claimed the cavalry had been surrounded by the Indians and a Little Bighorn scenario had ensued. Once the truth was revealed, the Indian children at the agency school became stricken with fear that their parents had been among those killed at Wounded Knee. The teachers summoned all the students back into the school. They feared that vengeful Indians at the agency would seek revenge by burning down the schoolhouse, so the presence of their children in the building would preclude any possibility of such an occurrence.

The Indians both straggling in to Pine Ridge and those already there were indeed incensed. Some sought to surround and attack the agency, but cooler heads prevailed. Others took off for

the Badlands. Some vengeful Brule and Oglala embarked to rescue their fellow Indians or join what was left of the fray at
Wounded Knee and were killed or wounded by cavalry. But Chief
Red Cloud and American Horse, who had befriended the white
man in his later years, worked to keep their fellow Indians calm.
So did Father John Jutz, who ran the Holy Rosary Episcopal
Mission four miles north of Pine Ridge. The sisters were given
the opportunity to join a convent in Omaha, but opted to stay
and help the victims of the tragedy.

Though often thought of as the last "battle" of the Indian Wars,
others of far less consequence ensued as early as that same week.
On December 30, 1890, one soldier was killed by Lakota that had
attacked a wagon train at White Clay Creek. Two days later, a
skirmish occurred between Indians and two companies of the
Sixth Cavalry.

"Peace on Earth, Good Will To Men"

Meanwhile, about fifty surviving Indians had been loaded into a
wagon and wheeled into Pine Ridge. After freezing in the open
wagon as an officer searched for shelter—the barracks were all
full with cavalry—they were placed on hay that had been scattered onto the floor of the Episcopal Church. The wounded were
later treated by army doctors, though many refused to allow a
man in uniform to tend to them, and some soon died. Those who
survived were given coffee and bread. A day later, a temporary
soup kitchen and bakery were opened and the Indians were provided some fresh beef. Ironically and sadly, strung across the
front of the pulpit was a banner that read "PEACE ON EARTH,
GOOD WILL TO MEN."[5]

Brule chief Two Strike and his men took Red Cloud prisoner
and spirited him away to the Badlands. They met up with Short
Bull, who had been on his way from the Badlands to Pine Ridge,
and informed him of the massacre at Wounded Knee. Red Cloud,
who wrote to the Indian Defense Association that the renegade
Indians decided they would die before returning to the agency,
added that he was told he would be killed if he attempted an
escape to Pine Ridge.

Meanwhile, many of the agency Indians who had been pacified over the years, accepting Christianity and the white man's way of life, told of their anger and bitterness over the recent events. Among them was schoolteacher Luther Standing Bear, who later expressed his fury.

"News arrived of the terrible slaughter of Big Foot's whole band," he wrote in his memoirs. "Men, women and children—even babies were killed in their mothers' arms! This was done by the soldiers. According to the white man's history this was known as the 'battle' of Wounded Knee, but it was not a battle—it was a slaughter, a massacre. Those soldiers had been sent to protect these men, women and children who had not joined the Ghost dancers, but they had shot them down without even a chance to defend themselves.

"When I heard of this, it made my blood boil. I was ready myself to go and fight them. There I was, doing my best to teach my people to follow in the white men's road—even trying to get them to believe in their religion—and this was my reward for it all! The very people I was following—and getting my people to follow—had no respect for motherhood, old age, or babyhood. Where was all their civilized training?"[6]

The same thought occurred to Dr. Charles Eastman, a converted Santee, who accompanied about one hundred civilians, including several reporters and a photographer, to Wounded Knee. He discovered to his horror dead bodies as many as three miles away, indicating that Indians had been hunted down and slaughtered. Some in his party saw dead relatives frozen on the ground, which caused great consternation. Eastman also saw a pile of about eighty bodies around the council fire and noticed that all were unarmed when they had been killed. The party did find a number of survivors who made their presence known by their wailing and moaning. One was a one-year-old baby who was well wrapped and miraculously unhurt. The girl was eventually adopted and educated by an army officer named L.W. Colby. Several other Indian orphans found homes in white families as well.

Indian scout Paddy Starr was placed in charge of organizing the burials, which began the day after the massacre. A total of

168 Miniconjou, including three pregnant women, were placed in a long trench that had been dug along a knoll at Wounded Knee. But the job was performed with little compassion. The bodies were piled up as stiff as cordwood on top of one another. They had been stripped naked by whites, who had joined the detail in order to add Ghost shirts to their memorabilia collections. Other articles of clothing and trinkets were sold in the nearby city of Chadron, Nebraska. *Chadron Democrat* reporter Charles Allen bought some of them and placed them on display in the window of the town bank. The sentiments of many whites were summed up by an editorial writer from that same newspaper, who wrote gleefully about the massacre in an article published on New Year's Day, 1891.

> "For once it has occurred that more Indians than soldiers have been slain, and we doubt not but that either General Miles or Brooke will be cashiered from the service as was General Harney for such pitiless bloodshed,"

he wrote.

> "Nothing will be done about the poor soldiers who were slain, but the Indian department is undoubtedly already getting in its work upon some crank of a congressman to present a bill before that august and wise [?] body to investigate the cause that led to the late massacre [?] and uncalled for [?] slaughter of such dear, good Indians as were 'Tomahawk That Kills,' 'Moon That Steals Horses,' 'Scalps All,' 'Eagle That Skins Alive,' 'Hawk Burns Alive,' 'Gall Wants All,' 'Buffalo That Kills The Babe' and a host more who are now really both *de facto* and *de jure* good Indians, not made so, however, by their religious training, but by good and well-directed shots and cuts late administered by Seventh and Ninth Cavalry.
>
> "We glory in the revenge of the Seventh, although they sustained a heavy loss, and notwithstanding there may have been a few in the late fight left who belonged to the Seventh during Custer's life, they nevertheless belong by name to a regiment which was at one time commanded by a soldier of national reputation as an Indian fighter and who, in 1876, with is entire command cut to atoms by Sitting Bull's warriors and probably participated in by several of the Big Foot gang

who bit dust a few days ago. We predict that the killing of Big Foot and his warriors will have a telling effect on the Messiah craze, and will civilize more reds who are yet alive than all the power of God and education that has been pumped into them for the past 16 years."[7]

Back to the Badlands

The soldiers killed at Wounded Knee were buried on December 31 amid freezing temperatures and howling, bitter winds. There would be no gun salute on that day because of the threat of an Indian attack, but the worries of the military were unjustified. The Indians on the way to the Badlands wanted nothing more to do with the white man. They had enough water and wood for shelter and they were also busy rounding up every piece of cattle in sight to provide a supply of meat for the winter. Those who held hope against hope in the power of the Ghost Dance danced. The Indians posted scouts at the entrance of the Badlands at all times to maintain their secrecy. But the army command understood that the about four thousand Lakota, including an estimated fifteen hundred warriors, were now well armed, well fed and willing to die.

Miles decided to preach patience. Though his soldiers could have outlasted the renegade Indians in another pitched battle, he didn't see the need to risk hundreds or even thousands more lives. He did, however, leave the warm surroundings of his Rapid City headquarters for Pine Ridge on New Year's Eve to formulate a plan. And that plan included his heading to the Badlands along with Brooke and the Second Infantry to take charge of the operation. The soldiers surrounded the Indians in an attempt to starve them into submission while working with them on a peaceful solution.

The days that followed brought more conflict. The two prominent protagonists in the latest drama were Army Lieutenant Edward Casey, an officer of Cheyenne scouts, and Brule warrior Plenty Horses, whose training at the Carlisle boarding school in Pennsylvania had left him bitter, as did the massacre, which motivated him to defiantly trade in his suit and cropped hair for a blanket, moccasins, braids, and war paint.

Casey's scouts served as a reconnaissance force with a cavalry squad led by Lieutenant George B. Sanford. They camped near the mouth of White Clay Creek, about eight miles away from the recalcitrant Indians. Units led by Generals Brooke and Miles were deployed to the east and west. Casey's Cheyenne scouts kept an eye on the Sioux village and met often with Lakota war- riors between their two camps. On January 6, several Lakota met with Casey, who sensed good intentions and a chance for a peaceful solution, so he decided to ride forth the following morn- ing to meet with Brule and Oglala leaders.

Among those on site was Plenty Horses, who was busily help- ing construct defenses against a military attack. He was among an estimated forty Sioux who met Casey and two Cheyenne scouts about two and a half miles north of the Stronghold. After the two exchanged handshakes and pleasant greetings, most of the Sioux rode off to join their comrades. Plenty Horses and sev- eral others continued their conversation with Casey and his scouts. Through interpreters, Casey convinced a Sioux named Bear Lying Down to ride back to the Stronghold with the mes- sage that the Army lieutenant wanted to meet with some of the chiefs, possibly even Red Cloud.

Casey then sent Cheyenne scout Rock Road back to White River, possibly to inform the soldiers of the peaceful intentions of a meeting, and slowly followed the trail of Bear Lying Down. Plenty Horses, who had learned to speak English at the Carlisle school, chatted with Casey as they rode toward the Stronghold along with fellow Sioux White Moon and Old Broken Arm.

When Bear Lying Down arrived, Red Cloud was holding coun- cil in his tipi, where the Indians were debating whether to accept Miles' invitation to return to Pine Ridge for peace talks. They had just decided to accept that invitation and meet with Miles the next day when Bear Lying Down arrived with Casey's mes- sage. Bear Lying Down was urgently warned that Casey needed to turn back because there were just enough angry warriors to all but ensure that he would be killed if he rode anywhere near the area. Pete Richard, who was Red Cloud's well-respected son- in-law, was dispatched to halt Casey in his tracks.

Richard spoke with Casey, who had traversed a mile closer to the Sioux camp. But as they spoke, a mounted Plenty Horses positioned himself a few feet behind Casey. Distraught and confused about being accepted neither in the white nor Indian world, Plenty Horses slid a Winchester out from underneath his blanket, placed it on his shoulder, killed Casey with a bullet that cleared through his head and rode off. The stunned Richard decided against killing Plenty Horses. He sent Bear Lying Down back to inform Red Cloud of Casey's death and forged ahead along with Cheyenne scout White Moon to report back to Brooke.

Despite the cold-blooded murder, Miles remained determined to bring the standoff to a peaceful conclusion. His patience was rewarded on January 15, 1891, when the Sioux leaders surrendered. What Kelley estimated as between five thousand and six thousand Indians, including eighteen hundred warriors, packed up four hundred seventy three tipis and marched back to Pine Ridge. Guns were willingly turned in.

Among those returning was Short Bull, who had lost all desire to fight. He understood the senselessness of battling superior forces. And he understood that the war between his people and the United States was over.

"During all this time my heart was bad, yet I did not want my people to fight the government," he said. "I might have done much harm but I always kept my people from it. I wanted no fighting. I wanted to do as the Messiah bid me. Some ten days afterwards a delegation was sent out to see us from General Miles, asking us to return to the agency so as to save any more bloodshed. General Miles sent to us several times, but we paid no attention, but now I told my people, 'Pack up everything you have and we will move toward the agency, and I hope we will be allowed to live there in peace. General Miles said we shall not be fired upon and I believe him."[8]

In the meantime, Miles tried to appease the Indians and further the cause of justice by setting the wheels in motion for a court-martial for Forsythe for the slaughter at Wounded Knee. He relieved Forsyth of his command of the Seventh Cavalry and ordered a Court of Inquiry investigation, claiming falsely that his actions were directed by President Benjamin Harrison. Miles received a telegraph from the Army stating that McKinley had no intention of having a Court of Inquiry case started against Forsyth, but Miles did so anyway on January 7, 1891.

Forsyth and his officers had an advantage in that they were the only people at Wounded Knee who were allowed to testify—the enlisted men were not. Indian survivors Frog and Celene Not Help Them also presented testimony, but not in person. Also testifying were civilians Wells and Episcopal missionary Charles Cook.

The primary thrust of the questioning revolved around whether the soldiers shot purposely at women and children. The officers continually claimed that their men avoided doing so to the best of their abilities, though such assertions were challenged repeatedly by Miniconjou and civilian witnesses.

Whitside did admit that his men couldn't avoid hitting women and children with their initial barrage of gunfire and that it was impossible to distinguish between male and female from afar after the Indians fled on horseback. Captain Myles Moylan claimed he heard officers scream out reminders not to shoot women and children. Many other officers concurred, stating that great precautions were taken to prevent casualties among such innocents. They even stated that they were successful in doing so despite evidence to the contrary. Captain Allyn Capron even suggested that it was impossible not to kill squaws who were engaging in sex with Indian men at the time of the shooting, adding his belief that some Miniconjou women and children must have been killed by their own people.

It is believed by many that the identical nature of the soldiers' testimony indicates that their stories had been prearranged. The army had previously contended that fewer than thirty Indian males has survived the initial attack—how, then, could the soldiers not recognize the women and children and why were so many murdered two or even three miles away from the scene?

Captain Frank Baldwin, one of two officers who presided over the Court of Inquiry, issued his final report upon the completion of testimony. He conceded that Forsyth and his men should have done a better job separating the Indians from themselves, an order from Miles that had been disregarded and could have avoided the tragedy. But in the end, Baldwin cleared Forsyth of all charges. Frustrated and angry, Miles added his own summation to the report, stating that the disposition of Forsyth's troops could hardly have been handled more poorly and that the massacre occurred despite evidence that plainly showed that most of the guns had been confiscated and the vast majority of the warriors were unarmed. He added that such circumstances precluded any possibility that the soldiers who claimed the Indians had shot their own men were speaking the truth.

Based on Forsyth's own estimation that 90 Lakota were killed at the council site and Miles' claim that there were only one hundred six warriors to begin with, the latter was justified in his concerns. If those numbers were indeed accurate, the soldiers spent hours in the morning and afternoon tracking down and killing about two hundred Indians, the vast majority of whom were women and children. Yet on February 4, 1891, Major General John Schofield rejected Miles' offerings in the official report and recommended not only that the case against Forsyth be dropped, but that he should be reinstated as Seventh Cavalry commander. Schofield stressed that the evidence showed the soldiers took great precautions to avoid killing women and children at Wounded Knee.

Not only did that end the investigation of the massacre—ignored were claims by Indians and some whites that drunkenness among the soldiers played a role in what was arguably the poor judgment that led to the tragedy—but a number of Seventh Cavalry men received Congressional Medals of Honor. Included were several who were awarded for "using every effort to dislodge the enemy" at the ravine, where so many Indians were killed.[9]

Further angering some Indians was the treatment of Plenty Horses. They assumed Casey's killer would be granted leniency since in the murder occurred in a time of great tension and peace had since been achieved. But white laws were different—after all, Casey was shot from behind with no chance to defend himself. Miles understood that an arrest would stir the emotions of some Indians, so he ordered that it be done quietly. Plenty Horses was seized by an army officer and a group of Oglala scouts in mid-February and taken into custody near Sturgis, South Dakota Two trials ensued and Plenty Horses was cleared of the charges and set free. Before he was acquitted, he confessed to the jury foreman that he killed Casey to be accepted again in the Indian community.

"I am an Indian," he said. "Five years I attended Carlisle and was educated in the ways of the white man . . . I was lonely. I shot the lieutenant so I might make a place for myself among my people. Now I am one of them. I shall be hung and the Indians will bury me as a warrior. They will be proud of me. I am satisfied."[10]

So was Miles, but for different reasons. In the 1920s, he expressed his optimism that the path laid down by the white man would lead to a seamless assimilation for Indians.

"It has been more than twenty years since [Wounded Knee], and not a hostile shot has been fired between the government forces and the Indians," he wrote. "Nearly all of the great warriors have passed on to the Happy Hunting Ground, and the young men of today have ceased to know even the skill and experience of the hunter and warrior. They have come up through the schools instead of the warpath. They have had the benefits of a life of civilization rather than the camp of Indian hostilities."[11]

Perhaps after centuries of warfare and dozens of massacres, Miles was merely attempting to justify the government treatment of Indians as a way to steer them toward what the white world in America considered civilization. Perhaps he truly believed in the righteousness of his thoughts and actions.

Notes

1. Frazer, Arnold Lt. Col. "Ghost Dance and Wounded Knee," *Cavalry Journal* 43 (1934): 18–20.

2. Coleman, William S.E. *Voices of Wounded Knee*. Lincoln, Nebraska: University of Nebraska Press, 2000. 301.

3. *Rapid City Daily Journal*, February 26, 1891.

4. Lindberg, Christer. "Foreigners in Action at Wounded Knee," *Nebraska History* 71 (Winter 1990): 170–181.

5. Brown, Dee. *Bury My Heart at Wounded Knee*. New York: Henry Holt and Company, 1970. 445.

6. Standing Bear, Luther. *My People the Sioux*. Lincoln, Nebraska: University of Nebraska Press, 1975. 223–224.

7. *Chadron (NE) Democrat*, January 1, 1891.

8. Coleman, William S.E. *Voices of Wounded Knee*. Lincoln, Nebraska: University of Nebraska Press, 2000. 373.

9. Yenne, Bill. *Indian Wars: The Campaign for the American West*. Yardley, PA: Westholme Publishing, 2006. 292.

10. Utley, Robert M. "The Ordeal of Plenty Horses," *American Heritage* Volume 26, Issue 1 (December 1974).

11. Miles, Nelson. *Serving the Republic: Memoirs of the Civil and Military Life of Nelson A. Miles, Lieutenant-General, United States Army*. Ithaca, N.Y.: Cornell University Library, 2009 (first published 1911) 245–247 [accessed November 2009]. http://books.google.com/books?id=6QOOlln2HMsC&printsec=frontcover&dq=Nelson+Miles:+Serving+the+Republic&source=bl&ots=IDHKMItfsh&sig=_b4LMt4QgfxXquE617FDGPIgFuI&hl=en&ei=PCtiS4etHZKKNI3u0OoL&sa=X&oi=book_result&ct=result&resnum=1&ved=0CAcQ6AEwAA#v=onepage&q=&f=false

---

SEVEN

Epilogue: The Siege at Wounded Knee, 1973

AMERICANS HAD TO WAIT FOR reports to trickle in to learn about the Wounded Knee massacre in the final days of 1890. But when a second incident occurred at that site, they could watch the proceedings on television.

Indeed, it took nearly a century following the tragedy of Wounded Knee for Indian militancy to be reborn—and the resurrection occurred on the same site.

Not so ironically, the protest movement that exploded into violence a few years later coincided with a time in American history when protests against the establishment and particularly the U.S. government had become commonplace. By the late 1960s, battles had been waged by antiwar factions against the military industrial complex, by blacks against longstanding racism, by women against traditional gender roles, and by gays against homophobia and laws that treated them like second-class citizens. It seemed far less surprising that Sioux anger and frustration would boil over during that era than it would have in previous or even future generations.

The seeds of what has been labeled Wounded Knee II were planted in 1968, the most divisive and violent year in American history since the Civil War. It was then that an organization called the American Indian Movement (AIM) was formed by a group of urban Indians in Minneapolis. In the 1950s and 1960s, more than half of all American Indians lived in major cities, the result of a government relocation program meant to further assimilate them into American culture with the promise of jobs and an education. More than one hundred thousand Indians were urbanized, but most didn't benefit socially or economically. The result was that many of them radicalized, leading to the birth of AIM and other albeit less militant groups.

Meanwhile, the Oglala Sioux at Pine Ridge were experiencing problems both on their reservation and in border towns. The troubles from within revolved around an iron-fisted tribal government head named Dick Wilson. Wilson not only gave jobs to friends and family members, but full-blooded Indians who remained loyal to tribal chiefs strongly believed he gave preferential treatment to those who were bi-racial and assimilated, such as himself. In his employ were Indians many Sioux deemed as "goons." Wilson's critics claimed that those who served as his protectors were quite willing to pummel anyone who threatened or criticized his leadership. In late 1972, the Oglala Sioux Civil Rights Commission was formed. It compiled stacks of evidence in an attempt to fight for Wilson's removal from office.

> "There's been a lot of accusations made here lately," Wilson said at the time. "One that upsets me is that I am using a goon squad. They are respectable and honest citizens of Pine Ridge."[1]

Increased Indian Militancy

Around that same time, AIM displayed its revolutionary spirit and militancy by taking over and occupying the Bureau of Indian Affairs in Washington for a week. Tensions were heightened in early 1973 when a white man killed an Indian in the town of Custer, which rests about fifty miles from Pine Ridge. Indian anger boiled over when the accused was charged with second-degree manslaughter rather than murder. About 200 angry protesters converged upon the town and engaged in a bloody, pitched battle with police when they were banned from the courtroom. The town was wrecked; the local Chamber of Commerce building was burned down, but the work of the AIM caught the attention of the Pine Ridge Indians. The militant group was summoned and soon it was decided that the appropriate retaliation for the murder would be a siege of the town of Wounded Knee, South Dakota. The town was located within the Pine Ridge Reservation, where the 1890 massacre occurred.

Soon two hundred male and female Oglala Lakota and AIM militants were driving into Wounded Knee armed with guns and Molotov cocktails. They stripped the only store, and then took over the church, holding the minister and other residents hostage while blocking all roads heading into town. They shot at authorities that arrived, which prompted the FBI to send in men to break up the roadblock. The protesters demanded that Wilson be fired, that a federal investigation be launched into corruption on the reservation, and that the Senate begin hearings into broken treaties made by the government with Indian nations. "We've got the whole Wounded Knee valley, and we definitely are going to hold it until death do us part," stated AIM leader Russell Means.[2]

The government rejected all the demands. The FBI brought in rifles while, as a show of force, Army planes began circling the area and armored personnel carriers rumbled in as well. The discrepancy in available technology was highlighted when a lone defiant Indian started shooting his pistol at the fighter jet. South Dakota senators James Abourezk and George McGovern, who had just finished his unsuccessful run for president, attempted in vain to mediate by promising to address the protesters' grievances if they surrendered. Members of AIM and other Indians refused categorically to yield before steps were taken to deal with the issues.

The standoff at Wounded Knee was of secondary importance to the heads of American state, who were far more concerned with the growing Watergate scandal that would eventually destroy the presidency of Richard Nixon. Negotiations at Wounded Knee continued, but the government refused to give in to any demands. By the end of the first week of the takeover, periodic gunfire was lighting up the night sky and three hundred FBI agents and U.S. marshals had been dispatched. Even Wilson's so-called goon squad, which was angry that the government didn't take more forceful military measures against the protesters, was creating roadblocks to provoke firefights. The government called upon AIM and its Indian allies to release the women and children, but that request too was ignored. The militants were ready for action. *Time* magazine correspondent Ken Huff reported what he witnessed:

"Seven Indian leaders stripped, some naked, others to their shorts, and entered an Indian sweat lodge—a wooden framework covered by an orange carpet and a purple blanket—to receive clarity of mind and body. The warriors, perhaps 150 of them, seemed perfectly willing to die. With the sun setting behind their backs and the chill wind whipping up puffs of dust, they formed a semicircle and watched as the tribal fathers emerged from the steaming lodge.

> "A Sioux spiritual leader named Leonard Crow Dog struck up a chant in the Lakota language. As each warrior passed by, he blessed him and painted a slash or a circle of red powder under the left eye. Each warrior then stepped into a white tepee, making a holy sign over the bleached skull of a buffalo head."[3]

The government then decided to take a more peaceful approach, lifting the roadblocks and forcibly sidelining Wilson and his men. But that only served to embolden the militants, who brought in more men and fresh supplies. When AIM leader Russell Means announced that Wounded Knee was now an independent Oglala nation and asked that three hundred thousand Indians from around the country join them, the government roadblocks returned. Finally, respected tribal leader Fool's Crow escorted a delegation to the United Nations to plead their case, but received no official recognition from the international organization.

Back at Wounded Knee, the AIM and reservation Indians were being taught the traditional ways of the Oglala tribe. Unlike other movements of the 1960s and early 1970s that espoused new and progressive thinking, the Indian movement embraced a return to tradition.

At the end of March, the U.S. Justice Department dispatched new negotiators and again changed its tactics. Both electricity and water were cut off at Wounded Knee and reporters that were giving the militants and their cause greatly desired publicity were sent packing. But they received great notoriety anyway when iconic actor Marlon Brando refused his Oscar at the Academy Awards, citing the negative and unrealistic portrayal of

Indians in American cinema. Brando sent Apache Indian actress Sacheen Littlefeather to the podium to personalize the protest. Meanwhile, polls revealed that most Americans sided with the protesters at Wounded Knee.

Under heavy pressure, the government quickly announced it had reached a deal with the Indians. It promised to investigate corruption on Pine Ridge while the Indians agreed to lay down their arms. But when the government demanded that the militants give up their guns first, the shaky agreement collapsed.

> "Do we give up our arms?" asked Means. "Hello! That is so stupid. It's beyond belief that they would even say that to the press. These stupid Indians are going to negotiate after they laid down their arms? What? Nobody does that in the entire world in history."[4]

Means was soon arrested. He spent the rest of the occupation in jail while the blockade of Wounded Knee resulted in many of the Indians becoming sick. Garbage began piling up and food was scarce. A cold snap struck the area, making the protesters even more uncomfortable. The militants were forced to call for a cutback to one meal a day, then a half-meal a day. Fortunately for them, a pilot friend of the AIM organized a food drop out of nearby Rapid City. More than two thousand pounds of food came out of the sky, prompting general shooting from the FBI.

Among the Indians outside the area that sympathized with the movement was a Cherokee named Frank Clearwater, who decided to join the fight at Wounded Knee along with his pregnant wife. During a firefight, Clearwater and others took refuge in the church. But a bullet tore through the plaster wall and hit him in the head. Though he had been at Wounded Knee for less than a day, he was rushed to the hospital and later died.

The killing heightened the government's anxiousness to end the siege. They gave Justice Department representative Kent Frizzell ten days to bring it to a peaceful and successful conclusion. But there would be no peace on April 26 when Oglala and Vietnam veteran Buddy Lamont emerged from safety to investigate upon hearing gunfire and was shot in the heart. Negotiators agreed to a ceasefire so Lamont could be buried at Wounded Knee alongside those who had been killed there eighty-three years earlier.

The End of the Struggle

By that time, Fool's Crow and many of the others had lost their will to fight. Though the AIM militants insisted on continuing the struggle, one and all gave up their arms on May 8. The seventy-one-day siege was over. The government promised to address their concerns, but little was done. Moreover, not only did Wilson remain in power, but he tightened his control while government officials did nothing. Over the next three years, his men killed two FBI agents and sixty AIM supporters. Hundreds of AIM members were brought to courts on minor charges, though most of the cases were dismissed. Still, the incident marked the end of AIM as an influential organization.

But though the siege of Wounded Knee proved fruitless in terms of making immediate political changes on the reservation, it increased awareness of Indian grievances, as well as their impoverished state, to the American public and it brought a sense of pride to tribes across the country. Indians began creating tribal schools in which they taught their children more traditional ways that would be passed on to future generations. In years past during the twentieth century, children were removed from their families and sent to boarding schools in which they were stripped of those traditions—as well as their Indian names—and forced to learn the ways of the white world.

Even the Supreme Court eventually recognized the unfairness of past treatment of the Sioux people. In 1980, it ruled that the federal government had taken Lakota land illegally and awarded the Indians $105 million. The Lakota refused the money, demanding land instead. The judgment later grew to $830 million. Seven years later, they and all other American Indian tribes received a judgment from the Supreme Court that allowed them to build and run gaming casinos in their land. The result of that ruling and the Indian Gaming Regulation Act of 1988 was the earning of billions of dollars by various tribes.

Though the Indians were never compensated for the land stolen from them in the nineteenth century, the Indian Gaming Regulation Act marked the first time that white America followed through with a promise that provided the tribes an opportunity to profit from their own territories.

There has been vastly increased awareness over the past half-century of the mistreatment of the Sioux and other nations during the Indian wars of well more than one hundred years ago, culminating in the slaughter at Wounded Knee. But perhaps because of their comparatively small population, the outcry against past discrimination of the Indians has paled in comparison to that in regard to African Americans, as a primary example. African Americans have made great gains in civil rights, particularly since the mid-twentieth century. But throughout U.S. history and to a great extent today, the Indians have been forgotten despite appalling unemployment rates and alcohol addictions of epidemic proportions. In that regard, it can be claimed that we as a nation learned virtually nothing from the Wounded Knee incident in 1890 aside from the fact that it was indeed a massacre, no matter how heavily armed the Lakota may or may not have been on that bloody morning.

The Lakota were discriminated against for the lifestyle they cherished and their refusal, rather than their desire, to fit in to white society. They were allowed to thrive as nomadic hunters until their lifestyle hindered U.S. expansionism and economic greed. When the Sioux finally succumbed to the overwhelming military force of expansionism, they were treated by many of those in power as second-class citizens.

Like many Native Americans, the Lakota never recovered economically and spiritually, though of course there are exceptions. According to the Harvard Project on American Indian Economic Development, the poverty rate for Native Americans, at 26 percent, is more than twice as high as that of the average American. In addition, the same study reported that the unemployment rate for Indians living on reservations was at 22 percent, four times that of the average American.[5] More disturbing was a 2005 North American Indian Housing Council study that revealed that those in tribes involved in the gaming industry had a 43 percent unemployment rate and the Lakota living on the Rosebud Indian Reservation in South Dakota were suffering from an 80 percent unemployment rate. The statistics were compiled before the recession that struck late that decade.[6]

The Wounded Knee massacre merely ended a military struggle, the result of which had been a foregone conclusion more than a decade before. The future of the Sioux and the many other Indian tribes across America cannot be accurately predicted. It has seemed inevitable for one hundred fifty years that their success could only be achieved by forging a path in the white man's world educationally, professionally, and socially. But in more recent years many Native Americans are returning to their roots. Some have discovered that they can indeed support themselves through profits earned by casinos on tribal land. The awareness of their heritage and pride in the past have come alive through tribal festivals and the National Museum of the American Indian in Washington, D.C., which opened in 2004, and various other Native American museums, such as the Mashantucket Pequot center in Connecticut. Though criticized for its militancy, the struggle by AIM in the early 1970s did help bring awareness to the current state of Indian affairs and a sense of pride to many Native Americans.

Notes

1. American Experience, "We Shall Remain: Wounded Knee," Episode 5. PBS Online [accessed January 2010]. http://www.pbs.org/wgbh/amex/weshallremain/

2. "Raid at Wounded Knee." *Time* magazine online, March 12, 1973 [accessed January 2010]. http://www.time.com/time/magazine/article/0,9171,944585,00.html

3. "PROTEST: A Suspenseful Show of Red Power." *Time* magazine online, March 19, 1973 [accessed January 2010]. http://www.timepi.com/time/magazine/article/0,9171,906923,00.html

4. American Experience, "We Shall Remain: Wounded Knee," Episode 5. PBS Online [accessed January 2010]. http://www.pbs.org/wgbh/amex/weshallremain/

5. John F. Kennedy School of Government, Harvard University. "The Harvard Project on American Indian Economic Development" [accessed January 2010]. http://www.hks.harvard.edu/hpaied/

6. North American Indian Housing Council. "Indian Housing Fact Sheet" [accessed January 2010]. http://www.naihc.net/news/index.asp?bid=6316

Biographies of Key Figures

Big Foot (ca. 1820–1890)

Though Hunkpapa chief Sitting Bull gained greater notoriety for his philosophical and spiritual leadership and Oglala warrior Crazy Horse for his exploits on the fields of battle, no Lakota played a more critical and, eventually, fatal role in the events surrounding the Wounded Knee massacre than Miniconjou leader Big Foot.

Though what is known about his early life is sketchy, it has been determined that Big Foot was born between 1820 and 1825 and was the son of Lone Horn. His Lakota name was Si Tanka (Spotted Elk). The Miniconjou tribe, known as "Planters by the River" was part of the Teton Lakota group that lived alongside the Hunkpapa in northwestern South Dakota. Big Foot was noted among his fellow tribesmen as an excellent hunter and horseman who owned a number of ponies that he had taken from Sioux enemies such as the Crow.

Upon the death of his father, Big Foot became chief of his tribe. He didn't share the warlike sentiments of some of his fellow Indians, opting most often to seek peaceful solutions, particularly in regard to quarrels with representatives of the U.S. government. Other Sioux bands often summoned him to use his talents as a mediator.

Big Foot and his Miniconjou, however, backed Sitting Bull, Crazy Horse, and other Lakota leaders in fighting the government after the Fort Laramie Treaty of 1868 had been broken and the Indians had lost much of their freedom and living space. But he did not participate directly in the Battle of the Little Bighorn in 1876. Following that great Sioux victory, his belief that his people should work toward adapting to the ways of the white man was strengthened. He encouraged them to toil the fields and send their children to schools being created for Lakota children.

Big Foot embraced the notion of blending in with white society and served as a delegate to Washington, D.C., where he spoke to the nation's leaders about Native American issues. He even worked to have a school built directly on the banks of the Cheyenne River Reservation in South Dakota, where his Miniconjou had been placed. The government tentatively agreed to build the school, but the matter was soon forgotten.

But though he continued to preach peace with the government and white settlers, his disenchantment with both grew with time. His band was ravaged by starvation and disease. Dishonest Indian agents, were stealing money appropriated for food and supplies. The government had worked to strip his people of their culture, even banning certain religious practices such as the Sun Dance.

Big Foot was among many Lakota who sought salvation. He immediately and fervently embraced the Ghost Dance, which he understood was intended to return his people to the lifestyle they enjoyed before the white man arrived. The unbearable conditions on the reservation motivated Big Foot and his band to practice the Ghost Dance beginning in the spring of 1890. But unlike other tribes, which sought violent retribution against the white man through the Ghost Dance, Big Foot continued to take a peaceful outlook. He felt the Ghost Dance would bring about freedom and return the wildlife back to the Plains so his Miniconjou could be hunters again.

After Sitting Bull resisted arrest and was killed on the Standing Rock Reservation, followers of the Hunkpapa chief joined Big Foot and his band at Cheyenne River. Big Foot feared that the government would attempt to arrest him as well, which motivated him to move his people to the Pine Ridge Reservation and link up with Chief Red Cloud. En route, he contracted pneumonia.

Though he had no intention of fighting, Big Foot and his Miniconjou were intercepted by the Seventh Cavalry and taken to Wounded Knee Creek. His confusing instruction to his braves on the morning of December 29, 1890, played a role in the massacre.

Big Foot at first advised against surrendering all the guns to the soldiers during a council meeting early that morning, but was later convinced to instruct his fellow Indians to give up their weapons. Minutes later Big Foot was gunned down along with an estimated three hundred Lakota. The photograph of Big Foot lying dead and frozen grotesquely on his back in the snow is among the most famous to have emerged from the massacre.

Crazy Horse (Tashunkewitko) (c. 1845–1877)

Crazy Horse spent much of his life fighting what seemed to be the inevitable U.S. encroachment on Lakota territory. His defiance and his prowess in battle, especially at the Battle of the Little Bighorn, made him, arguably, the greatest Sioux warrior in history. The monument of his likeness that is, as of this writing, being carved into the mountains of his beloved Black Hills speaks of the reverence both Indians and many whites have for Crazy Horse, who shares the distinction along with Sitting Bull as the most famous and admired Lakota of the nineteenth century.

The love Crazy Horse felt for the Black Hills can be traced to his birth around 1845 in that very area of what is now South Dakota. The young Oglala showed a distinct love for horses in the earliest days of his childhood, particularly after his father presented him with a pony of his own. He shadowed his father on buffalo hunts and eventually became well versed enough to participate. In an era before the Lakota used guns extensively, he gained a reputation as a talented marksman with his bow and arrow.

Crazy Horse and other young tribesmen often waited for young buffalo calves seeking their mothers to emerge from the field after hunts. He showed particular talent in re-enacting the chase, lassoing or driving the young animals into the camp. On one occasion he was challenged by the older boys to ride and remain on a large bull calf, which he did expertly.

At about the age of twelve, Crazy Horse experienced a vision he perceived as instruction as to how he must live the rest of his life. He saw himself as a humble and generous man who wore neither war paint nor decorations on his clothing. Though he blossomed into an accomplished warrior, he never boasted about his deeds and did indeed showed great benevolence, particularly in regard to his family. He proved himself to be dedicated to his fellow Lakota and their way of life.

His passion for family and Lakota traditions was matched by his hatred of whites he believed were bent on destroying both. His bitterness grew when daughter They Are Afraid Of Her died as a child from a disease passed on by white settlers. Another incident that had a profound effect on Crazy Horse stemmed from a relationship he had with a lover named Black Buffalo Woman, who was married to Oglala warrior No Water. In his mid-twenties, Crazy Horse stole Black Buffalo Woman away, prompting a jealous No Water to shoot him in the face. Crazy Horse later married Black Shawl.

Crazy Horse was too young to play a vital role in the negotiations between white commissioners and the Lakota when forts began appearing in their territory. His experience as a warrior had been limited to skirmishes against rival Indian tribes, but he agreed strongly with the view of chiefs who called for resistance. Though barely in his twenties, Crazy Horse participated in the highly successful and bloody attack on Fort Phil Kearny in 1866. In fact, he led a group of warriors in an attack on a contingent of Cavalry men busy chopping wood outside the fort, drawing soldiers out for an ambush. Lakota chief Sitting Bull took notice and anointed Crazy Horse as a principal war leader. Crazy Horse maintained a reputation as a man whose actions spoke louder than his words for the rest of his short life. He became not only a great warrior but aslo the tribe's most effective military strategist.

Those talents were put into use as battles against the U.S. Cavalry grew in frequency. They were most evident in the formation and execution of a plan that resulted in a slaughter of the Seventh Cavalry at Little Bighorn in 1876. He devised a strategy that allowed the Sioux and Cheyenne to surround General George Custer and his men, leading to the most lopsided and famous Indian victory in history.

Crazy Horse spotted Custer's regiment on the top of the bluff across from the river. He realized that the Cavalry plan was to attack the Indians on both sides, so he led his warriors north to cut the men off near the water. Soon the Cheyenne arrived to join the attack. Crazy Horse had outsmarted the Civil War general, who quickly met his demise along with all of his men.

Also meeting their demise, however, were the millions of buffalo that once roamed the plains and provided the Lakota with nearly everything they needed to sustain their freedom. Crazy Horse enjoyed his last moments of freedom in the months following Little Bighorn, but he was sometimes visited by Indian scouts in the employ of the government who finally convinced him to turn himself in to Fort Robinson in Nebraska with the promise of a fair trial. Crazy Horse was told that he and thousands of other Indians who also surrendered to authorities would receive an opportunity to tell their sides of the story. He spoke his mind with the following statement:

> "A very great vision is needed and the man who has it must follow it as the eagle seeks the deepest blue of the sky. I was hostile to the white man . . . we preferred hunting to a life of idleness on our reservation. At times we did not get enough to eat and we were not allowed to hunt. All we wanted was peace and to be left alone. Soldiers came and destroyed our villages. Then Long Hair (Custer) came. They say we massacred him, but he would have done the same to us. Our first impulse was to escape but we were so hemmed in we had to fight." [1]

Upon his arrival at Fort Robinson, Crazy Horse was angered to learn that General Crook had proclaimed as its Sioux leader Spotted Tail, who had ingratiated himself to white leaders over the past several years. Spotted Tail and other Indian scouts claimed to Crook that Crazy Horse was planning to murder the general and lead the Lakota into an insurrection. Upon learning of the treachery, Crazy Horse, who was also worried about his critically ill wife, proclaimed that only cowards commit murder. But the rumors about Crazy Horse motivated the government to arrest him. In the ensuing struggle against a guard at Fort Robinson, he was stabbed and killed at age thirty-five.

Despite the tender age in which he lost his life, he was revered in the memory of millions. Nearly seventy years later, at the same time the busts of four presidents were being sculpted into

Mount Rushmore, Lakota chief Henry Standing Bear requested that Crazy Horse be memorialized as well. He and several other Lakota asked renowned sculptor Korczak Ziolkowski to create a likeness of Crazy Horse in the Black Hills. Ziolkowski started the project before his own passing. The project to create the image of Crazy Horse on his horse, which is planned to be larger than the heads of the four Mount Rushmore presidents combined, is ongoing.

Note

1. Indigenous Peoples' Literature. "Crazy Horse/Tashunkewitko, Oglala" [accessed January 2010]. http://www.indians.org/welker/crazyhor.htm

Crook, George (1828–1890)

George Crook gained a reputation as an Indian fighter. He died with a reputation as an Indian protector.

Born into an Ohio farming family in 1828, Crook showed little early aptitude as a soldier. He graduated near the bottom of his class at West Point in 1852, after which he was dispatched to the Northwest as a lieutenant to fight against the Shoshone, Nez Perce, and other tribes of that region. He quickly gained an admiration for the Indians, as well as sympathy for their plight. He was angered that the U.S. government had broken many of the treaties it brokered with the Indians. Despite his political views, he led successful campaigns against the tribes, though he later expressed that he felt sympathetic for those against whom he was fighting.

Crook returned east upon the outbreak of the Civil War in 1861 and displayed superior military leadership. He was promoted to captain and served in such battles as the Second Bull Run and Chickamauga before being placed in command of the Army of West Virginia in 1864. He was captured by the Confederates in February 1865, but was freed a month later. He earned the rank of lieutenant colonel following the war and immediately was sent back to the Northwest to confront the Paiute for the next years. President Ulysses S. Grant, who was pleased with his work, placed him in charge of the Arizona Territory, where he was in charge of placing the Apache onto reservations.

That task would prove difficult. Crook established his willingness to use Indian scouts to track down his prey, but also showed that he preferred to use negotiation rather than warfare to settled differences. His newest task began with a 675-mile trek into Apache territory. Upon arriving at Camp Bowie, which was in the process of being constructed, he met with Apache chiefs, including Cochise, and was told they were not hostile and yearned to remain at peace.

Crook replied that he knew there was trouble between the Apache and the white man and that, whoever was to blame, it couldn't continue. He added that he was there to protect them from the white trouble makers, but only if the chiefs would do the same with Indians who raided and killed. But Crook also expressed his belief that with more white settlers on the way and the wild game disappearing, the Indians needed to adapt to the white world. He promised to find them work at wages comparable to those earned by whites.

He continued his peaceful approach to a successful conclusion. He subdued Chief Chalipan, who commanded more than two thousand Western Apaches, by promising work on an irrigation project and both a market and immediate payment for any crops raised by his tribe. Rather than wait for government action, Crook collected equipment from the camps and forts under his command and put the Apache to work on planting dozens of acres.

Meanwhile, Crook fought against Arizona whites who argued for Apache extermination, including a group of corrupt businessmen who sought to provoke the Indians into fighting whites so they could sell supplies to the military. Their efforts failed; by 1872 Cochise had signed a peace treaty. After Grant promoted him to brigadier general, Crook remained in Arizona for two years promoting better treatment of the Apache and other tribes of the region. He attempted in vain to have schools for Apache children opened in the belief that they should remain with their families rather than be shipped east to receive their educations.

Crook was sent east to the Plains in 1875, but any hope that he could solve peacefully the "Indian problem" there was quickly lost. He sought an end to tensions by ordering white gold seekers out of the Black Hills, which had been ceded to the Sioux in the Fort Laramie Treaty of 1868. That worked only briefly—the miners simply returned. Crook then followed orders when the government demanded that all Plains Indians turn themselves into reservations.

About fifty thousand renegade Indians remained free at the time and Crook's Seventh Cavalry regiment set out on March 1, 1876, to bring them in. He had some success with the Cheyenne, but not others. He understood that subduing the Sioux nation would require a Herculean effort, so he lured Indian scouts from such tribes as the Arapaho, Crow, Shoshone, and Ute for a military campaign that began on May 29. They marched along the Rosebud River as part of a three-pronged push into Wyoming and Montana territories. Regiments led by Generals Alfred Terry and John Gibbons were also on the way, but Crook became concerned because he had not heard from them.

On June 17, 1876, an Indian hunting party had spotted Crook and his men, and about five hundred Sioux and Northern Cheyenne warriors, including Sitting Bull and Crazy Horse, rode off to fight them. Crook's troops were startled when the Indian war party raced into the camp at Rosebud Creek camp and confused by the Indian tactic of moving from one spot to another between strikes. The cavalry could never get its footing to launch a defensive. In fact, Crook ordered a return to his base camp for reinforcements. As they waited for more troops, he received word of the slaughter of General Custer and his men in the Battle of the Little Bighorn. It has been claimed that Crook's inability to reach the site and help militarily doomed the Seventh Cavalry.

The overwhelming military response marked the end of the resistance of the Plains Indians. Crazy Horse was killed in 1877 and Sitting Bull and his band fled for Canada. By 1882, Crook was dispatched again to Arizona, where the Apache had fled their reservations and had resumed their guerrilla war against whites under Chiricahua tribe leader Geronimo, who played a cat-and-mouse game with Crook and his men. Geronimo retreated into the mountains time and again, leaving Crook frustrated. He was dismissed from his command in 1886, whereupon General Miles ended the stalemate by exiling Geronimo and his tribe to Florida.

Crook was promoted to major general and placed in charge of the Department of the Missouri in 1888, but he became sick and died of heart failure on March 2, 1890. It has been speculated that had the peaceful Crook remained in charge, the massacre at Wounded Knee would never have occurred. Among those who mourned his passing was Oglala chief Red Cloud, who stated that Crook had never lied to his people, but rather had given them hope. It was reported that the Apaches were so distraught that his scouts at the Camp Apache reservation formed a circle, bent their heads, and cried.

Gall (1840–1894)

No prominent Lakota can be identified more strongly with a con-version from anti-U.S. militancy to the embracing of the white way of life than the Hunkpapa leader Gall. Among the most active and violent supporters in the battle against the U.S. Army before and during the Battle of the Little Bighorn, and arguably the greatest warrior from chief Sitting Bull's band, Gall eventu-ally softened and thrived as a farmer.

Gall was born in 1840 along South Dakota's Moreau River in great proximity to where he was placed nearly four decades later on the Standing Rock Reservation. During his youth, he and his fellow Hunkpapa searched for buffalo along the vast plains. His father died young, which forced him to be raised by his mother, Walks-with-Many-Names. She received help in bringing up the child from various other relatives in the tribe. He thrived as both a hunter and warrior. His strength and barrel-chested physique soon became his defining physical characteristic.

He quickly attracted the attention of Sitting Bull, who was impressed with Gall's talents in competitions such as wrestling, javelin throwing, and pony riding, all of which were held to train Lakota in the art of warfare. Sitting Bull was so impressed with Gall's performance in battle against traditional enemies such as the Crow that he placed him into the exalted Strong Heart Society. But though he showed great promise as a warrior, Gall also gained recognition as a headman, or tribal peace leader. He was considered to be among the more demo-cratic of the headmen.

Gall fought with Sitting Bull in the Battle of Killdeer Mountain against Army soldiers in 1864 and stood firm with him against the Fort Laramie Treaty of 1868. He headed a delegation of Hunkpapa to a conference in July of that year to discuss its terms and told the commissioners that peace between his people and the United States would not be achieved until the government agreed to remove the military posts along the Missouri River. He did, however, eventually concede and signed the treaty.

When gold was discovered in the Black Hills and the government insisted that all Lakota return to the Great Sioux Reservation, a crisis ensued, resulting in the destruction of the Seventh Cavalry at Little Bighorn. Gall's wife and child were killed on the opening of hostilities, but he gathered himself to lead the Lakota into battle and play a critical role in their victory. Gall and Crazy Horse emerged as the greatest Sioux warriors of their time.

The military reaction to Little Bighorn forced Gall to retreat along with Sitting Bull and other Hunkpapa to Canada. But Gall boasted a more practical view than his chief and returned to the United States. six months before Sitting Bull, who felt abandoned. The relationship between the two soured. Gall saw no other option than to turn himself into Fort Buford, after which he was transported to the Standing Rock agency.

It was then he developed a relationship with Indian agent Major James McLaughlin that would change his life. McLaughlin gave Gall a sense of importance on the reservation by treating him as the leader of the Standing Rock Indians, even after Sitting Bull's arrival. McLaughlin believed Gall would not only accept assimilation into white culture, but would prove to be a positive role model for other reservation Indians.

He was right. Gall cooperated every step of the way with McLaughlin, becoming an assistant farmer in May 1883 and a district farmer four months later. He served in that same capacity until 1892 aside from a one-year stint as one of the Native American judges on the Court of Indian Offenses. He earned a reputation as being fair and compassionate, though McLaughlin felt he sometimes went overboard in his defense of Indians on trial and sometimes overruled the Hunkpapa leader.

Gall had lost his militancy by 1882, when the Edmonds Commission visited Standing Rock in a vain attempt to convince three-quarters of the Indians to sign a plan that was to divide the Great Sioux Reservation into six separate entities housing various tribes. Little did he or other Lakota that supported the plan know that the motive behind it was to provide land to white settlers. The U.S. Senate refused to ratify it because it failed to attract the signatures of three-fourths of the Indians, as had been agreed to by the Treaty of 1868.

Gall wasn't as open to the 1888 Dawes Act, which also provided for the partitioning of the Great Sioux Reservation. It stipulated that the government would own each individual piece of Indian land for twenty-five years and also made clear that leftover land would be sold to white settlers. The newly formed Pratt Commission arrived at Standing Rock to convince the Hunkpapa to sign, but on that issue Gall wouldn't be swayed. He refused to sign and urged his fellow Lakota to do the same.

The government understood that Gall's consent would be required to push through the Dawes Act, so he was invited to Washington via train along with other Sioux leaders. They were housed at the ritzy Belvedere Hotel and provided tours of such sites in the nation's capital as the Smithsonian Institute and the National Zoo. They also met with Secretary of the Interior William Vilas, who was supporting a clause in the bill that would give the Indians just fifty cents an acre for land that was worth more than twice that. Sitting Bull insisted on $1.25 per acre, which was agreed upon later when President Benjamin Harrison took office.

The newly formed Crook Commission was formed to again trek to the reservations and attempt to convince three-quarters of the Indians to sign. Gall was recalcitrant, but was convinced to affix his signature on the bill by McLaughlin. That was the final straw for Sitting Bull, whose disappointment with Gall was a partial motivation when the Hunkpapa chief uttered his legendary statement that there were no Indians left but himself.

Gall and his fellow Indians watched as they were deceived yet again. Surveys that were to determine individual Indian land were not taken before the Dawes Act became law. The beef allowance was also cut. A drought killed agricultural production and both starvation and disease overwhelmed the reservations.

The result was the embracing by many Indians of the Ghost Dance, which they believed would bring about salvation. Gall was among those during that period who feared militants such as Sitting Bull, so he asked McLaughlin to provide him and his Indian allies with weapons with which to defend themselves. The massacre at Wounded Knee made that unnecessary as most of the Ghost Dancers were slaughtered.

It has been reported that Gall was angered by the death of Sitting Bull at the hands of Indian agents, as well as the death of so many of his brethren at Wounded Knee. But rather than becoming belligerent, Gall faded into the background and avoided involvement in the post-massacre politics on the reservation. He concentrated on his work as a district farmer, which included teaching others how to most effectively work the land.

He also made a commitment to Christianity and education in the ways of the white man. The Episcopal clergy at the St. Elizabeth mission on the reservation educated his daughters. But he waited until 1892 to become baptized because he still embraced the spiritual teaching of his Hunkpapa ancestors. Two years later he married his fourth wife in a church, but he died less than a month after the ceremony, on December 5, 1894, of heart failure.

Those close to Gall believed his transformation from confirmed warrior to passive farmer who was committed to the white world was sincere and done with the best intentions for the Indian people in mind.

Miles, Nelson Appleton (1839–1925)

Nelson Appleton Miles played a critical role in the crushing of Indian resistance during the final quarter of the nineteenth century, though he later expressed an understanding and admiration for Native Americans that indicated a significant change of heart.

Miles was among millions of Americans whose personal desires and careers took them from east to west during the 1800s. He was born in Westminster, Massachusetts, on August 8, 1839, and quickly displayed a diligence and thirst for knowledge that would serve him well as an adult. During his youth he toiled at a crockery store and attended night school in Boston. He developed a keen interest in military affairs, poring over books about strategy and history. He yearned so desperately to forge a career as a soldier that he paid an old French officer to teach him the tricks of the trade.

He soon put his instruction to good use. He was commissioned as captain in the 22nd Massachusetts Volunteer Infantry Regiment when the Civil War began and immediately impressed his superiors with his work ethic, leadership abilities, and fearlessness. Miles performed so well in his first battle that he was promoted to lieutenant colonel, and then was upgraded to colonel and given the command of another volunteer army regiment during the Battle of Antietam in September 1862.

Miles earned further promotions for his bravery in battles at Fredericksburg and Chancellorsville at the height of the war, though he was wounded in the former. He was promoted again, this time to Brigadier General of Volunteers in 1864 after assuming charge of full divisions in Wilderness and Spotsylvania, two battles that helped decide the war in favor of the North. By the end of the conflict, he had participated in every major campaign aside from Gettysburg and had emerged as a national hero.

Controversy, however, would follow him throughout his career. His first encounter with it occurred in 1865 when he ordered Confederate President Jefferson Davis shackled in his cell to guard against a possible escape. Miles, who had befriended several men of great influence, finally landed the position of colonel in the regular army. Among those he befriended was legendary Civil War Major General William T. Sherman, whose niece, Mary Hoyt Sherman, he married on June 30, 1868. By that time, Miles had been transferred to the West, a move he at first resisted. In 1869, he was handed the command of the Fifth Infantry and thrust into the growing war between the United States and various Indian tribes, including the Sioux, Nez Perce, Cheyenne, Kiowa, Comanche, and Arapaho. During that time, his troops subdued such notable chiefs as Sioux Sitting Bull and

Crazy Horse, Nez Perce Joseph, and Apache Geronimo. Miles was promoted to brigadier general in 1880, after which he served six years as commander of the Department of the Columbia, Department of the Missouri, and Department of Arizona, where his most notable act was subduing and sending to Florida hostile Apache bands led by Geronimo.

After a brief stint heading the Department of the Pacific, Miles was dispatched to regain control of the Lakota Sioux. It was at that time he pulled the strings that led to the Wounded Knee massacre, ordering a halt to Ghost Dance activities considered a prelude to an Indian uprising. His report to the adjutant general thereafter indicated far less sympathy for the three hundred Indian dead at Wounded Knee than for the comparatively few perished soldiers from the Seventh Cavalry. He relieved Colonel. Forsyth from his command, charging him with gross negligence in the deaths of his fellow soldiers.

Miles was rebuffed as Forsyth was reinstated, but continued his military career, returning to command the Department of the Missouri in 1894. His stint at that post was distinguished by his strong reaction to the Pullman strike in Chicago, to which he sent troops.

A year later, he was named Commanding General of the Army and wrote a book titled *Personal Recollections and Observations of General Nelson A. Miles.* But his strongest desire, which was to become Secretary of War and even run for president, was thwarted due to a lack of support. Following that disappointment, he participated in the Spanish-American War and an invasion of Puerto Rico, which was overshadowed by his constant bickering with superior civilian officers. Though he was the top officer in the Army, he was given little authority by President William McKinley.

Miles felt unappreciated upon his retirement in 1903 when he received no message from President Theodore Roosevelt. He lived a quiet life thereafter, moving to Washington, D.C., and penning the book, *Serving the Republic* in 1911. In it, he expressed his admiration for the Lakota people and their way of life, both of which he helped eliminate in the late 1800s. Miles volunteered for the Army at age 78 when the United States joined World War I, but was turned down. He died from a heart attack in 1925 and was buried in the Arlington National Cemetery in a ceremony attended by President Calvin Coolidge.

Notes

1. Clemente, Luis. "Nelson Appleton Miles," The Spanish-American War Centennial Website [accessed January 2010]. http://www.spanam war.com/Miles.htm

2. Proctor, Redfield. "Col. Forsyth exonerated; his action at Wounded Knee justified. Decision of Secretary Proctor on the investigation—the colonel restored to the command of his gallant regiment," *New York Times*, Page 6. February 13, 1891 [accessed January 2010]. http://query.nytimes.com/mem/archive-free/pdf?res=9A03E7DA1F3BE5 33A25750C1A9649C94609ED7CF

Red Cloud (1819–1909)

No Lakota chief visualized the relationship between the U.S. government and his people with greater clarity than Red Cloud. A fierce warrior and talented military tactician while his Oglala and other tribes fought to maintain their independence, Red Cloud later accepted the helplessness of the situation and yielded to the majority and path of the Indians for success in the white world.

Red Cloud was at least a decade older than the other Lakota chiefs who distinguished themselves during the Indian wars of the late nineteenth century. He was born to an Oglala mother and Brule father around 1819 near the forks of the Platte River in Nebraska. He was quite young when his warrior father died, so he was raised by his maternal uncle, Chief Smoke. Among the last notable acts of his father was when he presented Red Cloud with a highly spirited colt.

> "My son," he said, "when you are able to sit quietly upon the back of this colt without saddle or bridle, I shall be glad, for the boy who can win a wild creature and learn to use it will as a man be able to win and rule men." [1]

Red Cloud practiced diligently throwing his lariat and soon mastered the art of lassoing the colt, though he was so small that he was dragged and lifted off his feet before he controlled it long enough to pitch it near the tipi. He was soon riding horse-back on short trips along with the older and bigger Oglala youth. The twelve-year-old Red Cloud had already shown enough talent in breaking horses to become one of the most successful young buffalo hunters of his tribe, though he admitted that his arrows didn't at that time penetrate deep enough into the thick hide of the animals to bring them down.

He was thrust into the role of warrior in battles against enemy neighboring tribes such as the Pawnee, Utes, Shoshone, and Crow at an early age. But it was the white man and white military leadership that by the late 1840s became a focus of his attention. In the late 1840s, his band was summoned by General Harney to discuss an agreement that would allow white settlers to move through Sioux territory. Though most of the Oglala rejected the notion, chief Bear Bull attempted in vain to convince them to accede to the request. Angered by his failure to do so, he fired at his own people and killed Red Cloud's brother and uncle. Red Cloud avenged the killings by shooting down Bear Bull, which brought him a great measure of respect from his fellow tribesmen. At the age of twenty-eight he was already a recognized leader.

His influence on head chief Man-Afraid-of-His-Horses and other Oglala, was significant particularly in regard to the growing tension between the Lakota and U.S. military. In 1854, young Oglala camped near Fort Laramie killed a cow for food that had been left off a Mormon emigrant train. The following day, thirty soldiers arrived at the Indian camp and demanded that the men who performed the act were to be arrested. In the ensuing battle, Red Cloud and his warriors killed every last man, even the interpreter. Retribution was expected but never came.

The struggles against white expansionism fostered a kinship between Indian tribes that had previously battled one another. When the Union Pacific was planning to build the transcontinental railroad through the heart of buffalo country, Red Cloud proved instrumental in bringing such Sioux tribes as the Oglala and Brule, as well as the Arapaho, Comanche, and Pawnee, together to form a united front. Many of those in the smaller tribes felt overcome by the wave of the future, succumbed to government pressure, and even became Indian scouts in the pay of the military. But a truce was generally observed—even the government hoped to put an end to tribal warfare. Red Cloud, however, stood fast against submission to government demands. He expressed his mistrust of the white man and his opposition to trading with them to his fellow Indians during one particular speech before an attack on Fort Phil Kearny in 1866.

"Hear ye, Dakotas!" he began. "When the Great Father in Washington sent us his chief soldier [General Harney] to ask for a path through our hunting grounds, a way for his iron road to the mountains and the western sea, we were told that they merely wished to pass through our country, not to tarry among us, but to seek for gold in the far west. Our old chiefs thought to show their friendship and good will, when they allowed this dangerous snake in our midst. They promised to protect the wayfarers.

> "Yet before the ashes of the council fire are cold, the Great Father is building his forts among us. You have heard the sound of the white soldier's ax upon the Little Piney. His presence here is an insult and a threat. It is an insult to the spirits of our ancestors. Are we then going to give up their sacred graves to be plowed for corn? Dakotas, I am for war!" [2]

Thus inspired, Sioux and Cheyenne warriors destroyed the fort and killed nearly one hundred of the inhabitants they had lured out. The government responded by offering the Fort Laramie Treaty of 1868, which created the Great Sioux Reservation, ceding them the Black Hills. Red Cloud was the last to sign—and only after all the forts standing on their territory had been removed.

But neither Red Cloud nor any other Plains Indian could stem the tide of white expansion. He saw just how enormous and powerful the United States. was on a trip to speak with national leaders in Washington, D.C., and sympathetic whites in New York City in 1870. While riding the "iron horse" he was overwhelmed by the sight of the white hordes and tall buildings in major cities such as Chicago and New York. He began to understand that resistance was futile.

When gold was discovered in the Black Hills in 1874 and prospectors streamed in from near and far in blatant violation of the Treaty of 1868, the government barely protested before opening the area up to the gold-seekers. It is unknown why Red Cloud didn't participate in the Battle of the Little Bighorn despite the fact that he remained adamant that the Lakota should resist all attempts to be subjugated to reservations in the midst of white infiltration into their sacred territory.

Just a few months following the crushing of the Seventh Cavalry at Little Bighorn, U.S. Army troops arrived to disarm Red Cloud and his Oglala band and escort them to Fort Robinson in Nebraska. They were then sent to the Pine Ridge agency, where he remained for the next thirty years as a reservation Indian. He still had his feisty moments, however, such as in 1880 when he claimed to a Yale University professor exploring the Badlands that there was political corruption at the agency. He continued to battle with Pine Ridge agent Valentine McGillycuddy over such issues as the distribution of government food and supplies, as well as the control of the Indian police force. His charges were deemed legitimate enough to launch an official investigation. His persistence even resulted in McGillycuddy's dismissal.

Red Cloud spoke strongly against Indian approval of the Dawes Act, which allotted Indian reservations into individual tracts. He didn't embrace the Ghost Dance movement of 1890, though he did invite Lakota who were harassed because they performed it to join him at Pine Ridge. He played no role in the Wounded Knee massacre of 1890, at which time he was over seventy years old. Red Cloud was nearly blind at the time of his death at age ninety in 1909.

The legendary chief is remembered as a courageous and noble warrior who accepted the inevitability of Indian assimilation into the white world, but could never be charged with being submissive.

Notes

1. Eastman, Charles A. "Red Cloud, as Remembered by Ohiyesa." *Indigenous Peoples Literature* [accessed January 2010]. http://www.indigenouspeople.net/redcloud.htm

2. Ibid.

Sitting Bull (Tatanka Iyotanka) (1831–1890)

Sitting Bull was not known for his skills as a warrior so much as for his role as the most respected philosophical and spiritual leader in the history of the Sioux nation. His vision and love for the Lakota way of life played the most critical role in the Sioux resistance to subjugation, and proved a motivation for Native Americans well past his death in 1890.

Sitting Bull was born the son of Chief Jumping Bull in a Hunkpapa village along the Grand River in what is now South Dakota in 1831. The site was known to his people as "Many Caches" for the number of food storage pits they had created. As a young boy he learned to use a bow and arrow, with which he hunted birds, rabbits, and various small creatures. Sitting Bull rode ponies and swam in the creek with other boys in the tribe. It was that atmosphere and freedom he would remain passionate about for the rest of his life.

Sitting Bull was given the name Tatanka Iyotanka, which describes a bull buffalo resting upon its haunches. He gained a reputation for performing tasks with great deliberation. He killed his first buffalo at age ten and four years later joined a raid against the Crow, who had been an enemy of the Lakota for generations and particularly for Sitting Bull, since it was a member of that tribe that killed his father. The 14-year-old officially became a Lakota warrior when he "counted coup," which was the act of touching an enemy warrior.

But it was his mind and spirit that brought respect from his fellow Hunkpapa. Sitting Bull not only became a leader of the Strong Heart warrior society, but also of the Silent Eaters, a group which discussed and took action in regard to the welfare of the tribe. He displayed a unique bravery and sense of honor during one particular battle against the Crow as a youth when he tossed an unarmed enemy his only loaded rifle and then attacked him with a stick. Sitting Bull was wounded, but managed to kill the Crow warrior.

The increasing contact with white settlers and soldiers that began in earnest in the early 1850s made an indelible mark on Sitting Bull. U.S. expansionism led to shrinking living space for the Lakota, broken treaties with the U.S. government, and the killing of millions of buffalo that once roamed the plains and served as the lifeblood of Sitting Bull's people. He joined the first battles against the U.S. Army in 1863 and participated in the Battle of the Killdeer Mountain a year later. He and his band led an unsuccessful raid of Fort Rice in 1865. He displayed courage in 1872 as part of a war party attacking white railroad workers near the Yellowstone River who were protected by soldiers. In the midst of the firefight with bullets whizzing by, the soldiers could see him leading several other warriors between the lines, sitting down, lighting a sacred pipe, and passing it around. Sitting Bull then calmly cleaned the pipe and strode off.

He understood from the horde of white settlers migrating west that his people could be overwhelmed in time, but he remained defiant. His anger grew after an expedition led by General Custer in 1874 revealed gold in the Black Hills, an area considered sacred by the Sioux nation. Prospectors flooded into the area with their picks and shovels in blatant disregard of the Fort Laramie Treaty of 1868, which had ceded the Black Hills to the Sioux. A year later, the federal government also shunned the agreement by opening it up to mining. Moreover, it was insisted that all Sioux outside the reservation by January 31, 1876, would be considered hostile. Sitting Bull knew a showdown was coming.

As three columns of federal troops converged, Sitting Bull convoked tribes of the Lakota, Cheyenne, and Arapaho to his camp along Rosebud Creek in Montana Territory. There they practiced the Sun Dance, during which time they had one hundred pieces of flesh slashed off their arms as a sacrifice to Wakan Tanka, the Great Spirit. It was at that time Sitting Bull received a vision of Bluecoats falling from the sky like grasshoppers into his camp. He predicted a great victory for his people.

Sitting Bull proved prophetic, though it was Lakota warriors Gall and Crazy Horse who led the fight. The Seventh Cavalry was surrounded and routed. During the battle, Sitting Bull tended to his family and then made medicine for the warriors. Though some accounts have contended that Sitting Bull was also involved in the hostilities, at age forty-five he was older than the Lakota who generally participated in battle. What is certain is that he spent some of his time during the Battle of the Little Bighorn protecting the women and children.

When the destruction of Custer and his men had been completed, Sitting Bull understood there would be retribution. The

Army pursued the Lakota across the Plains. Sitting Bull escorted a group of Lakota to Canada, where they remained for several years. He first refused an offer from General Alfred Terry to turn himself in to the reservation in return for a pardon for the actions at Little Bighorn. The Canadian government, however, was little help, and Sitting Bull surrendered at Fort Buford in Montana in 1881. Still proud and defiant, he expressed his pride that he was the last of his tribe to turn in his rifle. He asked for the freedom to travel to and from Canada, but was instead sent to the Standing Rock Reservation near his beloved Black Hills in 1883.

By the middle of that decade, some of the anger and resentment over the U.S. defeat at Little Bighorn had dissipated and Sitting Bull had become a revered figure. Buffalo Bill Cody took advantage of that by placing the Hunkpapa chief in his Wild West Show for four months in 1885. Sitting Bull was paid fifty dollars a week and anything he could earn through the signing of autographs, but he gave much of his money away to the raggedy children who befriended him before and after performances. He lamented the economic disparity in the white world, which heightened his sense of pride as a member of a Lakota community that made no distinction between rich and poor and, in fact, had little use for financial wealth.

Upon his return to Standing Rock, Sitting Bull lived in a cabin along the Grand River and sent his children to a nearby Christian school in the belief that future generations of Indians must learn to read and write. But he remained defiant, flouting the rules of the reservation, living with two wives, and always sending a family member to the agency for rations; he could not bring himself to directly receive rations from a government agency. One day he experienced a vision similar to the one that had foretold to him the defeat of the Bluecoats in 1876: he claimed a bird informed him that he would be killed by his own people. That too would prove prophetic.

Sitting Bull met his end at the height of the Ghost Dance movement. Though he questioned its effectiveness, he embraced the practice as something distinctly Indian. He had, after all, chastised his fellow Native Americans two years earlier for agreeing to the proposed Dawes Act, which separated the Lakota on the reservations and provided more land for white settlers. Though he was warned as an Indian leader to stop his tribe members from performing the Ghost Dance, which was greatly feared by some white citizens, Indian agents and government officials, Sitting Bull refused.

The end came just as Sitting Bull predicted. At first he planned to succumb to his arrest when Indian policemen confronted him at his home at Standing Rock on December 15, 1890, but he eventually heeded calls from his people to resist and became more defiant. A short gunfight ensued, which cost him his life. He was buried at Fort Yates in North Dakota, but in 1953 his remains were moved by descendants to a gravesite overlooking the Missouri River in Mobridge, South Dakota.

Primary Documents

1. *Harper's Weekly*'s Account of the 1862 Santee Slaughter

The first mass killing in the war between the U.S. Army and Sioux tribes occurred in Minnesota in the winter of 1862.

The Santee had grown weary and angry over the lack of food and supplies that had been promised them by the government. Some even began to starve, which was the plan as expressed by Indian agent Thomas Galbraith, who reiterated the government's intention to force the Indians into a white lifestyle by holding back provisions.

By 1862, the approximately six thousand six hundred Santee had lost patience. One day they confronted Galbraith about why they weren't receiving food despite well-stocked shelves at the store. Andrew Myrick, who was responsible for food distribution, replied curtly that if the Indians wanted to eat, they could eat grass.

The Santee proceeded to go on a rampage, killing more than one thousand white Minnesotans, including Myrick. Army troops commanded by Colonel Henry H. Sibley were summoned and successfully subdued the Santee, taking about two thousand prisoners in the process.

After the violence had subsided but before some of the Indians were hanged in the largest public execution in American history, the highly popular magazine Harper's Weekly *submitted the following report from an unnamed man who had accompanied a boy into the prison where the captured Santee were being housed. The account represented the general view of white settlers toward the American Indian during that period, particularly after the massacre:*

WE publish on page 801 a very striking picture of the identification of an INDIAN MURDERER (one of the leaders of the late

Indian foray into Minnesota) by a boy survivor who witnessed the massacre. The gentleman who made the sketch from which our picture is taken kindly sends us the following account:

"After fighting two severe battles, the troops under the command of Brigadier-General Sibley succeeded in capturing the greater portion of the bands who committed the recent murders. The victims amounted in number to over one thousand, and many no doubt are still lying in the woods, where they fled for shelter and were struck down. There is no record of a massacre so thorough in detail in the history of our country, fruitful as it is of Indian outbreaks. A short time since I was at South Bend, on the Minnesota River, and saws the captives. They are confined in strong log prisons and closely guarded, not so much to prevent their escape as to secure them from the vengeance of the outraged settlers. They are the most hideous wretches that I have ever seen. I have been in the prisons of Singapore where the Malay pirates are confined—the Dyacks, who are the most ferocious and blood-thirsty of their kind—but they are mild and humane in appearance compared to these Sioux warriors.

"Quite an incident occurred while I was there. A boy who had escaped after seeing the murder and outrage of his mother and sisters was brought in to look at the prisoners, and, if possible, identify them. One of the friendly Indians, who had distinguished himself by his bravery and humanity, accompanied the party to act as interpreter. When we entered the log-house that served for a prison the captives were mostly crouched on the floor, but of them arose and confronted us with a defiant scowl. Another, supporting himself on his arm, surveyed the party with a look like a tiger about to spring. The boy advanced boldly, and pointed him out without hesitancy. Subsequent investigation showed that his wretch had murdered eleven persons. The boy's eyes flashed as he told the sickening tale of his mother's murder, and the spectators could scarce refrain from killing the wretch on the spot. He never relaxed his sullen glare, and seemed perfectly indifferent when told of his identification by the interpreter.

"The entire country steams with slaughter, and there is scarce a family in the large district that was the scene of the outbreak that has not lost a member; and many are entirely cut off, and nothing left to indicate their fate but their devastated homes and the chance admissions of the prisoners.

"It will be long before the frontiers of Minnesota will recover from this tragedy, and many of the sufferers will seek justice with their ready rifles, and will range the vast plains west to the Missouri, until they have hunted every Indian into the mountains."

Source "The Indian Murderers in Minnesota." *Harper's Weekly.* (December 20, 1862): 807. [Accessed December 2009]. http://www .sonofthesouth.net/leefoundation/civil-war/1862/december/minnesota-sioux-massacre.htm

2. Fort Laramie Treaty of 1868

The Sioux signed many treaties, later broken, with the U.S. government. One of the most impactful, a treaty that planted the seeds of the subjugation of the tribes, was the Fort Laramie Treaty of 1868. The document set the tone for the conflicts within the Indian community and between the Indians and the government for years to come. Though many of the tribespeople succumbed to reservation life immediately, thousands of others resisted and became more militant in their desire to remain free.

The agreement was intended to end the nomadic lifestyle enjoyed by the Indians for centuries, tying them to reservations. The treaty allowed them to leave reservations for hunting purposes, but that right would also be eventually taken away from them. The motivation of the U.S. government was to provide small tracts of land to Indians in an attempt to transform them into farmers, a vocation in which they were wholly inexperienced and greatly impassionate. Indian children were also to attend schools, where they would learn the ways of the white world.

The Treaty of 1868 ceded great expanses of land to the Sioux, including the coveted Black Hills. But when gold was discovered in those hills, the government refused to stop the flood of settlers and miners in blatant disregard to the agreement. And as time went by, the acreage given to Indians both individually and collectively continued to shrink.

So did the hunting grounds, also in direct violation of the treaty. White hunters riding through on railroads killed millions

of buffalo for hides and for sport in the years following the sign-ing of the agreement, destroying the Sioux way of life. White set-tlers also brought diseases that took a heavy toll on the Indian population.

Those who ignored or refused to sign the Treaty of 1868 brought themselves into direct conflict with the U.S. Army, bringing about the Indian Wars of the late nineteenth century. These conflicts were heightened by the Battle of the Little Bighorn in 1876 and punctuated by the Wounded Knee Massacre in 1890. The impor-tant points of the treaty read as follows:

Lieutenant General William T. Sherman, General William S. Harney, General Alfred H. Terry, General O.O. Augur, J.B. Henderson, Nathaniel G. Taylor, John G. Sanborn, and Samuel F. Tappan, duly appointed commissioners on the part of the United States, and the different bands of the Sioux Nation of Indians, by their chiefs and headmen, whose names are hereto subscribed, they being duly authorized to act in the premises.

ARTICLE I.
From this day forward all war between the parties to this agree-ment shall for ever cease. The government of the United States desires peace, and its honor is hereby pledged to keep it. The Indians desire peace, and they now pledge their honor to main-tain it.

If bad men among the whites, or among other people subject to the authority of the United States, shall commit any wrong upon the person or property of the Indians, the United States will, upon proof made to the agent, and forwarded to the Commis-sioner of Indian Affairs at Washington city, proceed at once to cause the offender to be arrested and punished according to the laws of the United States, and also reimburse the injured person for the loss sustained.

If bad men among the Indians shall commit a wrong or depreda-tion upon the person or property of nay one, white, black, or In-dian, subject to the authority of the United States, and at peace therewith, the Indians herein named solemnly agree that they will, upon proof made to their agent, and notice by him, deliver up the wrongdoer to the United States, to be tried and punished according to its laws, and, in case they willfully refuse so to do, the person injured shall be reimbursed for his loss from the annuities, or other moneys due or to become due to them under this or other treaties made with the United States; and the President, on advising with the Commissioner of Indian Affairs, shall prescribe such rules and regulations for ascertaining damages under the provisions of this article as in his judgment may be proper, but no one sustaining loss while violating the provisions of this treaty, or the laws of the United States, shall be reimbursed therefor.

ARTICLE II.

The United States agrees that the following district of country, to wit, viz: commencing on the east bank of the Missouri river where the 46th parallel of north latitude crosses the same, thence along low-water mark down said east bank to a point opposite where the northern line of the State of Nebraska strikes the river, thence west across said river, and along the northern line of Nebraska to the 104th degree of longitude west from Greenwich, thence north on said meridian to a point where the 46th parallel of north latitude intercepts the same, thence due east along said parallel to the place of beginning; and in addition thereto, all existing reservations of the east back of said river, shall be and the same is, set apart for the absolute and undisturbed use and occupation of the Indians herein named, and for such other friendly tribes or individual Indians as from time to time they may be willing, with the consent of the United States, to admit amongst them; and the United States now solemnly agrees that no persons, except those herein designated and authorized so to do, and except such officers, agents, and employees of the government as may be authorized to enter upon Indian reservations in discharge of duties enjoined by law, shall ever be permitted to pass over, settle upon, or reside in the territory described in this article, or in such territory as may be added to this reservation for the use of said Indians, and henceforth they will and do hereby relinquish all claims or right in and to any portion of the United States or Territories, except such as is embraced within the limits aforesaid, and except as hereinafter provided.

ARTICLE III.

If it should appear from actual survey or other satisfactory examination of said tract of land that it contains less than 160 acres of tillable land for each person who, at the time, may be authorized to reside on it under the provisions of this treaty, and a very considerable number of such persons shall be disposed to commence cultivating the soil as farmers, the United States agrees to set apart, for the use of said Indians, as herein provided, such additional quantity of arable land, adjoining to said reservation, or as near to the same as it can be obtained, as may be required to provide the necessary amount.

ARTICLE IV.

The United States agrees, at its own proper expense, to construct, at some place on the Missouri river, near the centre of said reservation where timber and water may be convenient, the following buildings, to wit, a warehouse, a store-room for the use of the agent in storing goods belonging to the Indians, to cost not less than $2,500; an agency building, for the residence of the agent, to cost not exceeding $3,000; a residence for the physician, to cost not more than $3,000; and five other buildings, for a carpenter, farmer, blacksmith, miller, and engineer—each to cost not exceeding $2,000; also, a school-house, or mission building, so soon as a sufficient number of children can be induced by the agent to attend school, which shall not cost exceeding $5,000.

The United States agrees further to cause to be erected on said reservation, near the other buildings herein authorized, a good steam circular saw-mill, with a grist-mill and shingle machine attached to the same, to cost not exceeding $8,000.

ARTICLE V.

The United States agrees that the agent for said Indians shall in the future make his home at the agency building; that he shall reside among them, and keep an office open at all times for the purpose of prompt and diligent inquiry into such matters of complaint by and against the Indians as may be presented for investigation under the provisions of their treaty stipulations, as also for the faithful discharge of other duties enjoined on him by law. In all cases of depredation on person or property he shall cause the evidence to be taken in writing and forwarded, together with his findings, to the Commissioner of Indian Affairs, whose decision, subject to the revision of the Secretary of the Interior, shall be binding on the parties to this treaty.

. . .

ARTICLE VII.

In order to insure the civilization of the Indians entering into this treaty, the necessity of education is admitted, especially of such of them as are or may be settled on said agricultural reservations, and they, therefore, pledge themselves to compel their children, male and female, between the ages of six and sixteen years, to attend school, and it is hereby made the duty of the agent for said Indians to see that this stipulation is strictly complied with; and the United States agrees that for every thirty children between said ages, who can be induced or compelled to attend school, a house shall be provided, and a teacher competent to teach the elementary branches of an English education shall be furnished, who will reside among said Indians and faithfully discharge his or her duties as a teacher. The provisions of this article to continue for not less than twenty years.

ARTICLE XI.

In consideration of the advantages and benefits conferred by this treaty and the many pledges of friendship by the United States, the tribes who are parties to this agreement hereby stipulate that they will relinquish all right to occupy permanently the territory outside their reservations as herein defined, but yet reserve the right to hunt on any lands north of North Platte, and on the Republican Fork of the Smoky Hill river, so long as the buffalo may range thereon in such numbers as to justify the chase. And they, the said Indians, further expressly agree:

1st. That they will withdraw all opposition to the construction of the railroads now being built on the plains.

2d. That they will permit the peaceful construction of any railroad not passing over their reservation as herein defined.

3d. That they will not attack any persons at home, or travelling, nor molest or disturb any wagon trains, coaches, mules, or cattle belonging to the people of the United States, or to persons friendly therewith.

4th. They will never capture, or carry off from the settlements, white women or children.

5th. They will never kill or scalp white men, nor attempt to do them harm.

6th. They withdraw all pretence of opposition to the construction of the railroad now being built along the Platte river and westward to the Pacific ocean, and they will not in future object to the construction of railroads, wagon roads, mail stations, or other works of utility or necessity, which may be ordered or permitted by the laws of the United States. But should such roads or other works be constructed on the lands of their reservation, the government will pay the tribe whatever amount of damage may be assessed by three disinterested commissioners to be appointed by the President for that purpose, one of the said commissioners to be a chief or headman of the tribe.

7th. They agree to withdraw all opposition to the military posts or roads now established south of the North Platte river, or that may be established, not in violation of treaties heretofore made or hereafter to be made with any of the Indian tribes.

ARTICLE XV.

The Indians herein named agree that when the agency house and other buildings shall be constructed on the reservation named, they will regard said reservation their permanent home, and they will make no permanent settlement elsewhere; but they shall have the right, subject to the conditions and modifications of this treaty, to hunt, as stipulated in Article XI hereof.

ARTICLE XVI.

The United States hereby agrees and stipulates that the country north of the North Platte river and east of the summits of the Big Horn mountains shall be held and considered to be unceded Indian territory, and also stipulates and agrees that no white person or persons shall be permitted to settle upon or occupy any portion of the same; or without the consent of the Indians, first had and obtained, to pass through the same; and it is further agreed by the United States, that within ninety days after the conclusion of peace with all the bands of the Sioux nation, the military posts now established in the territory in this article named shall be abandoned, and that the road leading to them and by them to the settlements in the Territory of Montana shall be closed.

Source PBS: New Perspectives on the West, "Archives of the West: 1856–1868." [Accessed January 2010]. http://www.pbs.org/weta/thewest/resources/archives/four/ftlaram.htm

3. Red Cloud's 1870 Cooper Institute Speech

As the 1870s approached, most Sioux didn't understand the extent of U.S. encroachment. What they knew about the white man had been learned through their relations with whites on a comparatively small geographic scale.

But when Red Cloud rode the "Iron Horse" to Washington, he began to realize the enormity of what was ninety years later described by President Dwight Eisenhower as the military-industrial complex, as well as the overwhelming number of whites who populated what any Plains Indian would have perceived as gigantic cities.

It was a humble yet proud Red Cloud who met with leaders in the nation's capital and then accepted an invitation to speak in New York City in June 1870. The speech he made to mostly sympathetic whites at the Cooper Institute in the nation's largest city was conciliatory and intended to tug on the heartstrings and play to the logic of his listeners. Red Cloud hoped to convince the audience that the depiction of his people coming from the media was unbalanced.

Red Cloud was not the only Sioux to foray into the white world during the latter half of the nineteenth century; fifteen years later Sitting Bull traveled with Buffalo Bill Cody's Wild West Show. But Red Cloud gained more sympathy from whites during his short trip to Washington and New York than any Indian of that era through his kind approach and heartfelt comparisons between the

lives led by technologically advanced whites and his compara-
tively primitive Native Americans.

Red Cloud asked for the support of the white people who gath-
ered to hear him speak in New York. But little could be done to
stem the tide of white expansionism. His words were nevertheless
embraced by the New Yorkers, who rose to their feet to give Red
Cloud a standing ovation upon its conclusion. It was spoken in
its entirety as follows:

My Brothers and my Friends who are before me today: God almighty has made us all, and He is here to hear what I have to say
to you today. The Great Spirit made us both. He gave us lands and
He gave you lands. You came here and we received you as brothers. When the Almighty made you, He made you all white and
clothed you. When He made us he made us with red skins and
poor. When you first came we were very many and you were few.
Now you are many and we are few. You do not know who appears
before you to speak. He is a representative of the original American race, the first people of this continent. We are good, and not
bad. The reports that you get about us are all on one side. You
hear of us only as murderers and thieves. We are not so. If we had
more lands to give to you we would give them, but we have no
more. We are driven into a very little island, and we want you, our
dear friends, to help us with the Government of the United States.
The Great Spirit made us poor and ignorant. He made you rich
and wise and skillful in things which we knew nothing about. The
Good Father made you to eat tame game and us to eat wild game.
Ask anyone who has gone through to California. They will tell you
we have treated them well. You have children. We, too, have children, and we wish to bring them up well. We ask you to help us do
it. At the mouth of Horse Creek, in 1852, the Great Father made a
treaty with us. We agreed to let him pass through our territory
unharmed for fifty-five years. We kept our word. We committed no
murders, no depredations, until the troops came there. When the
troops were sent there trouble and disturbance arose. Since that
time there have been various goods sent from time to time to us,
for only once did they reach us, and soon the Great Father took
away the only good man he had sent us, Colonel Fitzpatrick. The

Great Father said we must go to farming, and some of our men went to farming near Fort Laramie, and were treated very badly indeed. We came to Washington to see our Great Father that peace might be continued. The Great Father who made us both wishes peace to be kept; we want to keep peace. Will you help us? In 1868 men came out and brought papers. We could not read them, and they did not tell us truly what was in them. We thought the treaty was to remove the forts, and that we should then cease from fighting. But they wanted to send us traders on the Missouri. We did not want to go on the Missouri, but wanted traders where we were. When I reached Washington the Great Father explained to me what the treaty was, and showed me that the interpreters had deceived me. All I want is right and justice. I have tried to get from the Great Father what is right and just. I have not altogether succeeded. I want you to help me get what is right and just. I represent the whole Sioux nation, and they will be bound by what I say. I am no Spotted Tail, to say one thing one day and be bought for a pin the next. Look at me. I am poor and naked, but I am the Chief of the nation. We do not want riches, but we want to train our children right. Riches would do us no good. We could not take them with us to the other world. We do not want riches, we want peace and love.

The riches that we have in this world, Senator Cox said truly, we cannot take with us to the next world. Then I wish to know why commissioners are sent out to us who do nothing but rob us and get the riches of this world away from us? I was brought up among the traders, and those who came out there in the early times treated me well and I had a good time with them. They taught us to wear clothes and to use tobacco and ammunition. But, by and by, the Great Father sent out a different kind of men; men who cheated and drank whisky; men who were so bad that the Great Father could not keep them at home so sent them out there. I have sent a great many words to the Great Father but they never reached him. They were drowned on the way, and I was afraid the words I spoke lately to the Great Father would not reach you, so I came to speak to you myself; and now I am going away to my home. I want to have men sent out to my people whom we know and can trust. I am glad I have come here. You belong in the East and I belong in the West, and I am glad I could come here and that we could understand one another. I am very much obliged to you for listening to me. I go home this afternoon. I hope you will think of what I have said to you. I bid you all an affectionate farewell.

Source "The Great Chief: Red Cloud Meets His White Brethren at Cooper Institute." *New York Times* (June 17, 1870): 1 [accessed December 2009]. http://query.nytimes.com/mem/archive-free/pdf?_r=1&res=9801E7DD1F3 CE13BBC4F52DFB066838B669FDE

4. *New York Times* Account of the Battle of the Little Bighorn

The Battle of the Little Bighorn, in 1876, arguably did more to anger and frighten white America than any event in U.S.-native relations. Though it was provoked by the U.S. government and the cavalry that had been dispatched to the area, the slaughter of General George Custer and his men alarmed the white citizenry, particularly in that region. The Sioux and Cheyenne won the battle, but the U.S. government, spurred by public outrage and fear, was determined from that moment forward to subdue the Indians by whatever means deemed necessary.

That outrage and fear grew as reports trickled in and were published in various newspapers and journals of the day. It often took more than a week for the full story to be reported in major cities in the east. Most were slanted against the Indians, though they also conceded the recklessness of Custer in ordering his men into a battle with such a large number of Sioux warriors.

The number of Indians involved in the Battle of the Little Bighorn was often exaggerated, as the following article that appeared in the New York Times *attests. But aside from such inflated numbers and anti-Indian tone that one would gather from the use of such terms as "red devils" to describe the Sioux, the dispatches received and written were largely accurate.*

DISPATCHES FROM GEN. TERRY RECEIVED AT SHERI-DAN'S HEADQUARTERS: THEORIES OF THE BATTLE—PROBABLY TEN THOUSAND SIOUX IN POSITION—THE ATTACK CONDEMNED AS RASH BY OFFICERS OF EXPE-RIENCE—DISPOSITION OF THE WOUNDED.

Chicago, July 6.—At the headquarters of Lieut. Gen. Sheridan this morning, all was bustle and confusion over the reported massacre of Custer's command. Telegrams were being constantly received, but most of them were of a confidential nature and withheld from publication. It is known that the unfortunate command broke camp on the North Rosebud on June 22 for the purpose of proceeding in a direction which would bring it to the point named about the 25th, at which place a bloody fight is reported to have taken time. The following dispatch, the last received at headquarters in this city previous to the news of the massacre, confirms the accounts given to the extent of showing that Custer intended to go to that place.

Camp on the North Rosebud, June 21, 1876.

Lieut. Gen. P.H. Sheridan, Commanding Military Division of the Missouri, Chicago: No Indians have been met with as yet, but traces of large and recent camp have been discovered twenty or thirty miles up the Rosebud. Gibbon's column will move this morning, on the north side of the Yellowstone, for the mouth of the Big Horn, where it will be ferried across by the supply steamer, and whence it will proceed to the mouth of the Little Horn, and so on. Custer will go up the Rosebud tomorrow with his whole regiment, and thence to the headwaters of the Little Horn, thence down the Little Horn.

A. H. TERRY,

Brigadier General Commanding.

A dispatch received at the quarters of Gen. Sheridan this morning at 11 o'clock confirms the first reports received. The dispatch states that the forces were falling back, and that the wounded had been sent to Fort Lincoln. No details were given, but the officers at headquarters regard it as a full confirmation of the engagement reported. In reply to an inquiry as to whether the attack was made by Gen. Custer of his own accord, or under orders from the department, an answer was given that Custer made the charge of his own volition. A still later dispatch from Lieut. Kinzie, of the Seventh Cavalry, was received asking that he be transferred from the department where he is now on duty to the scene of action. This is also regarded as another confirmation of the bloody massacre reported. Gen. Custer's family are at Fort Lincoln, to which point the wounded are being conveyed.

So far as an expression in regard to the wisdom of Gen. Custer's attack could be obtained at headquarters, it was to the effect that Custer had been imprudent, to say the least. It is the opinion at headquarters among those who are most familiar with the situation, that Custer struck Sitting Bull's main camp. Gen. Drum, of Sheridan's staff, is of opinion that Sitting Bull began concentrating his forces after the fight with Crook, and that no doubt, Custer dropped squarely into the midst of no less than ten thousand red devils and was literally torn to pieces. The movement made by Custer is censured to some extent at military headquarters in this city. The older officers say that it was brought about by that foolish pride which so often results in the defeat of men. It seems that a few days before Gen. Terry had offered four additional companies to Custer, but that officer refused them.

The information at headquarters further is to the effect that Gen. Gibbon with his force was known to be moving up to Custer for the purpose of reinforcing him; and that he knew of this, and knew that Gibbon would arrive by the following day after the engagement. I have it on as good authority as one of the leading officers at headquarters, that Custer had been ordered by Terry to make a march toward the Little Big Horn and to form a junction with a column of infantry that was moving diagonally across the country to the same point. The two columns were then to cooperate and make an attack. Instead of marching from twenty to thirty miles per day, as ordered, Custer made a forced march and reached the point of destination two or three days in advance of the infantry; then finding himself in front of the foe he foolishly attempted to out his way through and punish the red devils.

Source "Confirmation of the Disaster." *New York Times.* (July 6, 1876). Little Bighorn Project: Newspaper Articles [accessed January 2009]. http://littlebighornproject.com/id31.html

5. A Newspaper Article About the Death of Sitting Bull

The cultural differences between U.S. and Indian civilization, particularly those of the traditional Sioux, was vast throughout most of the nineteenth century. Though many Americans felt or even expressed their sympathies over the plight of the natives, others thought of them as nothing more than savages.

That held true for the media as well. Even a chief as respected by his fellow Sioux and some in the white world as Sitting Bull was reviled by many newspaper writers. The death of Sitting Bull in mid-December 1890 prompted some to express their views that the final hurdle to civilizing the savage redskin had been eliminated.

Many in the media believed in Manifest Destiny, the theory that the white race was deemed by Providence to control the North American continent. The term, in fact, was coined in 1845 by journalist John L O'Sullivan, who was referencing what he perceived as the inalienable right of the United States to annex Texas, but it was later used to describe the righteousness of taking over the lands of Native Americans.

The last chief to stand in the way of achieving that goal was Sitting Bull. And in the days following his death, editorial writers who embraced what they perceived as the need for Indians to be assimilated into white culture wrote cheerily about his demise. Included was one from the St. Louis Republic, *who crafted the following:*

The death of Sitting Bull removes one of the obstacles to civilization. He was a greasy savage, who rarely bathed and was liable at any time to become infected with vermin. During the whole of his life he entertained the remarkable delusion that he was a free-born American with some rights in the country of his ancestors. Under this delusion, when civilized immigrants pushed over the Black Hills country in search of gold he considered them trespassers on the lands of his people and tried to keep them out. He was engaged in this absurd and wicked attempt when General Custer surprised his camp in the interests of civilization. Unfortunately for civilization General Custer was mistaken in the number of the savages who had assembled to fight for the land, which they foolishly believed was their birthright, and "a massacre" ensued. That is, it was one of those rare occasions when savagery for the moment had the best of it in a pitched battle with civilization. It was, of course, only for the moment, and Sitting Bull and his followers, who might have been easily and legally hanged as murderers, were granted a temporary respite.

This graciousness of the Great Father they have constantly abused by obstructing civilization in every possible way, especially in the worst way possible by trying to keep their land in a state of barbarism, and by insisting on their own understanding of treaties, regardless of necessary changes in translation into a highly civilized language, and of necessary amendments made in Congress. They have gone on holding ghost dances, complaining about the rations issued to them under treaties, objecting to the way their money was handled by the government, and it is charged on excellent civilized authority, actually stealing from civilized people who have settled on their lands.

Under such circumstances there could have been only one ending for Sitting Bull, and now that it has come he has no complaint to make. There is every reason to believe, therefore, that it was perfectly satisfactory to him. He himself had recognized it as inevitable and had fully made up his mind to it, preferring it to death in what in his barbaric way he called the "stone houses of the Great Father," meaning thereby the penitentiaries in which the Great Father, with the aid of Hon. Powell Clayton, Hon. Poker J. McClure and others of his Sanhedrin, attempts on occasion to incarcerate those who disagree with him in such a way as to inconvenience him.

So when Sitting Bull was surprised and overpowered by the agents of the Great Father, he set his greasy, stolid face into the expression it always took when he was most overcome by the delusion that he was born a native American from native American ancestry. Disarmed and defenceless [*sic*] he sat in the saddle in which he had been put as a preliminary to taking him to prison, and without a change of countenance urged his hand-ful of greasy followers to die free. This idiotic proceeding he kept up until he was shot out of the saddle.

So died Sitting Bull. So was removed one of the last obstacles in the path of progress. He will now make excellent manure for the crops, which will grow over him when his reservation is civilized.

The work of redeeming these excellent lands from barbarism has now reached a point where it can be at once carried to com-pletion. The filth and vermin-infested Sioux and other savages who have pretended a desire to live even under starvation rations and broken treaties will be persuaded by Sitting Bull's example, and a little skillful management of the same kind which converted him from a brutal savage into a good Indian, to stand up where they can be shot out of the way of advancing progress.

Mr. Harrison should continue to act with the same promptness and firmness he has shown in Sitting Bull's case. While one of these barbarians lives to claim an acre of unentered land in the United States he will remain as an obstacle to progress. A firm persistence by the President in the admirably progressive policy he has illustrated in Sitting Bull's case will make good Indians of all the rest of them, bucks, *squaws* and *pappooses*. And the future historian will say of them, no doubt, that they died justly, because they owned lands and would not use fine-toothed combs.

Source "The Last of Sitting Bull." *St. Louis Republic.* (December 17, 1890). First Nations. [Accessed January 2010]. http://www.dickshovel .com/greasy.html

6. Views of the Indian Wars from L. Frank Baum

Easily the most famed newspaper columnist covering the events of the Indian Wars of the late nineteenth century was L. Frank Baum, although he wasn't particularly famous at the time.

Baum gained notoriety in later years for authoring the child-ren's classic, The Wonderful Wizard of Oz, *which was published*

in 1900. The book, of course, was transformed in 1939 into the Wizard of Oz, *arguably the most beloved film in American history.*

The young Baum boasted a rather strange view of U.S.-Indian relations. He conceded that the Sioux had been wronged by the government for many years and, because of it, called for the annihilation of the tribe. He claimed that what he considered to be weak and indecisive government policy was to blame for the bloodshed at Wounded Knee, but he wasn't decrying the death of an estimated three hundred Indians, but rather the killing of comparatively few soldiers.

Baum crafted many editorials for the Aberdeen Saturday Pioneer *on the military struggles between the cavalry and the Sioux. The following appeared a few days after the events of Wounded Knee. In it, he claimed that the Sioux could never be transformed into civilized people and that steps should have been taken long before to kill them off before the lives of white soldiers were endangered.*

The peculiar policy of the government in employing so weak and vacillating a person as General Miles to look after the uneasy Indians, has resulted in a terrible loss of blood to our soldiers, and a battle which, at its best, is a disgrace to the war department. There has been plenty of time for prompt and decisive measures, the employment of which would have prevented this disaster. The *Pioneer* has before declared that our only safety depends upon the total extirmination [*sic*] of the Indians. Having wronged them for centuries we had better, in order to protect our civilization, follow it up by one more wrong and wipe these untamed and untamable creatures from the face of the earth. In this lies future safety for our settlers and the soldiers who are under incompetent commands. Otherwise, we may expect future years to be as full of trouble with the redskins as those have been in the past. An eastern contemporary, with a grain of wisdom in its wit, says that "when the whites win a fight, it is a victory, and when the Indians win it, it is a massacre."

Source Baum, L. Frank. *Aberdeen Saturday Pioneer.* (January 3, 1891). "L. Frank Baum's Editorials on the Sioux Nation: The Wounded Knee Editorial." [Accessed January 2010]. http://www.history.ox.ac.uk/

hsmt/courses_reading/undergraduate/authority_of_nature/week_7/
baum.pdf

7. Dewey Beard's Memories of Wounded Knee

Among the most vocal and visible Sioux survivor of the Wounded Knee massacre was Dewey Beard. Talking about the event was perhaps the only way he felt he could deal with the slaughter, which claimed the lives of his father, mother, two brothers, wife, and child.

Known as Wasee Maza (Iron Tail), Beard was eighteen years old when he participated in the Battle of the Little Bighorn, though he didn't arrive until it had nearly ended. He was thirty-three when most of his family members were wiped out at Wounded Knee.

He was known only as Iron Tail until many years following the massacre, when he was invited to Washington by General Nelson Miles and introduced to some U.S. military officials, including Admiral George Dewey, a naval hero from the Spanish-American War. Iron Tail was so impressed with Dewey that he incorporated his Sioux nickname (Beard) with the admiral's first name and adopted it for himself.

The events of Wounded Knee were kept alive by Dewey Beard and other survivors on both sides for decades. Years after the massacre, the last Lakota survivor of both Custer and Wounded Knee talked at length about the fight inside the council grounds, about the flight from the Miniconjou village into the ravine. Beard was among the most aggressive Indians during the fight and managed to kill a number of soldiers. He spoke through an interpreter, who both summarized and quoted him directly, starting with the fight over the gun of Black Coyote, which went off to set off disaster:

[Interpreter:]

"The struggle for the gun was short, the muzzle pointed upward toward the east and the gun discharged. In an instant a volley followed as one shot, and the people began falling. He saw everybody was rolling and kicking on the ground. He looked southeastward and he did not know what he was going to do. He had only one knife. He looked eastward and saw the soldiers were firing on Indians and stepping backwards and firing. His thought was to rush on the soldiers and take a gun from one of them. He rushed toward on the west to get a gun. While he was running, he could see nothing for the smoke; through the rifts he could see the brass buttons of the uniforms; he rushed up to a soldier whose gun rested over Dewey's shoulder and was discharged when the muzzle was near his ear, and it deafened him for a while. Then he grabbed the gun and wrenched it away from the soldier. When he got the gun, he drew his knife and stabbed the soldier in the breast . . . While Dewey was on this soldier, some other soldiers were shooting at him, but missed him and killed soldiers on the other side. When he got up he ran right through the soldiers toward the ravine, and he was the last Indian to go into the ravine. The soldiers were shooting at him from nearly all directions, and they shot him down . . . Dewey tried to get to the ravine and succeeded in getting on his feet . . . Right on the edge of the ravine on the south side were soldiers shooting at the Indians who were running down into the ravine, the soldiers' shots sounded like fire crackers and hail in a storm; a great many Indians were killed and wounded down there . . .

"When he went to the bottom of the ravine, he saw many little children lying dead in the ravine. He was now pretty weak from his wounds. Now when he saw all those little infants lying there dead in their blood, his feeling was that even if he ate one of the soldiers, it would not appease his anger . . . The Indians all knew that Dewey was wounded, but those in the ravine wanted him to help them. So he fought with his life to defend his own people. He took his courage to do that—"I was pretty weak and now fell down.' A man with a gunshot wound through the lower jaw had a belt of cartridges, which he offered Beard and asked to try and help them again."

[Beard, through the interpreter:]

"'When he gave me the cartridges, I told him I was badly wounded and pretty weak, too. While I was lying on my back, I looked down the ravine and saw these women, girls and little girls and boys coming up. I saw soldiers on both sides of the ravine shoot at them until they had killed every one of them."

[Interpreter:]

"He saw a young woman among them coming and crying and calling, 'Mother! Mother!' She was wounded under her chin, close to her throat, and the bullet had passed through a braid of her hair and carried some of it into the wound, and then the bullet had entered from the front side of the shoulder and passed out the back side. Her Mother had been shot behind her. Dewey was sitting up and he called to her to come to him. When she came close to him, she fell to the ground. He caught her by the dress and drew her to him across his legs. When the women who the soldiers were shooting at got a little past him, he told this girl to follow them on the run, and she went up the ravine.

"He got himself up and followed up the ravine. He saw many dead men, women, and children lying in the ravine. When he went a little way up, he heard singing; going a little way farther, he came upon his mother who was moving slowly, being very badly wounded. She had a soldier's revolver in her hand, swinging it as she went. Dewey does not know how she got it. When he caught up to her she said, 'My son, pass by me; I am going to fall down now.' As she went up, soldiers on both sides of the ravine shot at her and killed her."

[Beard, through the interpreter:]

"I returned fire upon them, defending my mother. When I shot at the soldiers in a northern direction, I looked back at my mother and she had already fallen down. I passed right on from my dead mother and met a man coming down the ravine who was wounded in the knee . . ."

[Interpreter:]

"Dewey was wounded so that his right arm was disabled; he placed the thumb of his right hand between his teeth and carried his Winchester on his left shoulder, and then he ran towards where he has heard that White Lance [Dewey's brother] was killed. As he ran, he saw lots of women and children lying along the ravine, some alive and some dead. He saw some young men just above, and these he addressed, saying to them to take courage and do all they could to defend the women. 'I have,' he said, 'a bad wound and am not able to defend them; I could not aim the gun,' and so he told the young men this way. It was now in the ravine just like prairie fire when it reaches brush and grass . . . ; it was like hail coming down; an awful fire was concentrated on them now and nothing could be seen for the smoke. In the bottom of the ravine, the bullets raised more dust than there was smoke, so that they could not see one another.

"When Dewey came up into the 'pit,' he saw White Lance upon top of the bank, and was rolling on down towards the brink to get down into the ravine. He was badly wounded and at first was half dead, but later revived from his injuries. When Dewey went into the 'pit,' he found his brother

William Horn Cloud lying or sitting against the bank shot through the breast, but yet alive; but he died that night."

[Dewey, through the interpreter:]

"Just when I saw my wounded brother William, I saw White Lance slide down the bank and stand by William. Then William said to White Lance, 'Shake hands with me, I am dizzy now'"

[Interpreter:]

While they had this conversation, Dewey said, 'My dear brothers, be men and take courage. A few minutes ago, our father told us this way, and you heard it. Our father told us that the all people of the world born of the same father and mother, when any great tragedy comes, it is better that all of them should die together than that they should die separately at different times, one by one . . .'

"White Lance and William shook hands. Then White Lance and Dewey lifted their brother up and stood him on his feet; then they placed him on White Lance's shoulder. White Lance was wounded in several places and weak from loss of blood, but he succeeded in bearing William to the bottom of the ravine . . . Dewey said they now heard the Hotchkiss or Gatling guns shooting at them along the bank. Now there went up from these dying people a medley of death songs . . . Each one sings a different death song if he chooses. The death song is expressive of their wish to die. It is also a requiem for the dead . . ."

[Dewey, through the Interpreter:]

"At this time, I was unable to do anything more and I took a rest, telling my brothers to keep up their courage."

[Interpreter:]

"The cannon were pouring in their shots and breaking down the banks which were giving protection to the fighting Indians . . . The Hotchkiss had been shooting rapidly and one Indian had gotten killed by it. His body was penetrated in the pit of the stomach by a Hotchkiss shell, which tore a hole through his body six inches in diameter. The man was insensible, but breathed for an hour before he died . . . In this same place there was a young woman with a pole in hand and a black blanket on it. When she would raise it up, the soldiers would whistle and yell and pour volleys into it. One woman here spoke to Beard and told him to come in among them and help them. He answered that he would stay where he was and make a fight for them; and that he did not care if he got killed, for the infants were all dead now, and he would like to die among the infants. When he was saying this, the soldiers were all shooting furiously . . . Dewey laid down again in the same little hollow and reloaded his gun. The soldiers across from him were shooting at him while he was reloading. While he was reloading, he heard a horseman coming along the brink of the ravine—could hear the foot falls. This man as he came along gave orders to the men which he supposed were to fire on the women in the pit for a fusillade was instantly opened on them . . .

"The sun was going down; it was pretty near sundown . . . He saw five Oglala Sioux on horseback. He called them, but they were afraid and ran away, but he kept on calling and going till they all stood still and he came upon them. He went on with them a little way and soon he met his brother Joseph coming toward them on horseback. Dewey asked, 'Where are you going?' Joe answered, 'All my brothers and parents are dead, and I have to go in and be killed, too; therefore I have come back.' Dewey said, 'You better come with us; don't go there; they are all killed there,' and the five Oglalas joined with Beard in the same appeal. Now the Oglalas left these two brothers. The Joe got off his horse and told Dewey to get on. Dewey was covered with blood. He mounted the horse and Joe walked along slowly. After a little, a mounted Indian relation came up behind them. The three went together over to White Clay Creek . . .

"Dewey's little infant, Wet Feet, died afterwards in the next March. This child was nursing its dead mother who was shot in the breast. It swallowed blood and from this vomited and was never well, was always sick till it died."

Source "A Massacre Survivor Speaks." [Accessed January 2010]. http://www.dickshovel.com/DwyBrd.html

8. Wovoka's Message About the Ghost Dance

Also known as Jack Wilson, the Paiute medicine man Wovoka became ill while doing heavy chores in a Nevada desert and fell into a trance on New Year's Day, 1899. He believed he was in contact with God and Jesus, who were angry over the way the white man had treated the Indians. The spirit world also told Wovoka that God was going to kill off the white man from the continent and resurrect the dead Indians and the wildlife that had disappeared from their territory. According to Wovoka, if the Indians rejected all white ways but treated them well, the performance of a Ghost Dance would result in such a metamorphosis.

Wovoka considered himself the messenger of God's word. He taught the Ghost Dance to many tribes throughout the west, but various interpretations followed. The Sioux believed that if they wore Ghost Shirts, the bullets of white soldiers couldn't hurt them. Wovoka later claimed that he never made such an assertion.

Several months after the Wounded Knee massacre, writer and ethnologist James Mooney embarked on a journey for the Bureau of American Ethnology to learn more about the dance that had played a significant role in costing hundreds of Indian lives. He received a copy of Wovoka's message by a Cheyenne named Black Short Nose, who had visited Wovoka, along with other Cheyenne and Arapaho to visit Wovoka. The medicine man delivered his message orally, but it was transcribed by a member of that delegation who had attended the Carlisle Indian school. The inclusions within the brackets were added by James Mooney in "The Ghost Dance-religion and the Sioux Outbreak of 1890, 14the Annual Report of American Ethnology in 1896."

The report reads as follows:

When you get home you must make a dance to continue five days. Dance four successive nights, and the last night keep up the dance until the morning of the fifth day, when all must bathe in the river and then disperse to their homes. You must all do in the same way.

I, Jack Wilson, love you all, and my heart is full of gladness for the gifts you have brought me. When you get home I shall give you a good cloud [rain?] which will make you feel good. I give you a good spirit and give you all good paint. I want you to come again in three months, some from each tribe there [the Indian Territory].

There will be a good deal of snow this year and some rain. In the fall there will be such a rain as I have never given you before.

Grandfather [a universal title of reverence among Indians and here meaning the messiah] says, when your friends die you must not cry. You must not hurt anybody or do harm to anyone. You must not fight. Do right always. It will give you satisfaction in life. This young man has a good father and mother. [Possibly this refers to Casper Edson, the young *Arapaho* who wrote down this message of Wovoka for the delegation.]

Do not tell the white people about this. Jesus is now upon the earth. He appears like a cloud. The dead are still alive again. I do not know when they will be here; maybe this fall or in the spring. When the time comes there will be no more sickness and everyone will be young again.

Do not refuse to work for the whites and do not make any trouble with them until you leave them. When the earth shakes [at the coming of the new world] do not be afraid. It will not hurt you.

I want you to dance every six weeks. Make a feast at the dance and have food that everybody may eat. Then bathe in the water. That is all. You will receive good words again from me some time. Do not tell lies.

Source New Perspectives on the West. "Archives of the West: 1887–1914." PBS.org. Wovoka's Message: The Promise of the Ghost Dance [accessed January 2010]. http://www.pbs.org/weta/thewest/resources/archives/eight/gdmessg.htm

9. The Defense of Colonel Forsyth

The accounts of what happened at Wounded Knee differ greatly. There are significant discrepancies between the testimonies of U.S. soldiers and the statements of surviving Indians and white civilian witnesses.

Secretary of War Redfield Proctor authored the following account of the tragedy, which appeared in The New York Times. *It differed from other descriptions of Wounded Knee in its claim that the soldiers were merely defending themselves against an Indian onslaught.*

The beginning of the article, which is not printed below, states the case of General Nelson Miles, who initiated a Court of Inquiry

against the actions of Colonel Forsyth, who was commanding the troops. Miles' contention was that Forsyth did not have his men properly disposed for avoiding casualties. But the investigation perpetrated by Proctor, which included no testimony of Indians, motivated the Secretary of War to exonerate Forsyth.

The conclusions reached by Proctor make claims that have been asserted as false by the vast majority of non-military surviving witnesses, including reporters, white civilians, and Miniconjou. The specific contentions are cited throughout the following article:

Gen. Schofield, commanding, submitted the case to the Secretary of War, with the following indorsement [sic]:

"The interests of the military service do not, in my judgment, demand any further proceedings in this case nor any longer continuance of Col. Forsyth's suspension from the command of his regiment.

"The evidence in these papers shows that great care was taken by the officers and generally by the enlisted men to avoid unnecessary killing of Indian in the affair of Wounded Knee and shows that the conduct of the Seventh Cavalry under very trying circumstances, was characterized by excellent discipline and in many cases by great forbearance. In my judgment the conduct of the regiment was well worthy of the commendation bestowed upon it by me in my first telegram after the engagement."

The [reports of the investigation] were returned to the Major General commanding with the following indorsement [sic] from the Secretary of War.

From the testimony taken by Major Kent and Capt. Baldwin, two officers of General Miles's staff, ordered by him to investigate the night at Wounded Knee, it appears that before the action Big Foot's band had been joined by Sitting Bull's following, and these bands embraced the most fanatical and desperate elements among the Sioux. They surrendered because of the necessities of their situation rather than from a submissive spirit. It was the sullen and unwilling yielding of a band of savage fanatics, who were overmatched and out of food, to superior force. It was not in good faith on the part of the younger braves, at least, but not yet with any definite pre-arranged plan of treachery. The surrender was made to Major Whitside, commanding the First Battalion of the Seventh

Cavalry, on the afternoon of Dec. 28. Col. Forsyth was ordered up to his support, and arrived at 8:45 o'clock that evening.

It was manifestly an imperative necessity to prevent the escape of any of these desperadoes during the process of disarming, or as a consequence, of the attempt to disarm them, for such escape would probably have resulted in a destructive raid upon the settlements. The troops appear to have been well disposed to prevent an outbreak which was not and could hardly have been anticipated by anyone under the circumstances, even in dealing with Indians, and the dispositions appear to have had the desired effect of convincing at least a majority of the Indians of the futility of any attempt to escape. If treachery was premeditated by any of the Indians, which seems extremely improbable, the majority of them were deterred from attempting to execute it until incited by the speech of the ghost dancer. The disarmament was commenced and it was evident that the Indians were sullenly trying to evade the order. To carry out this order the men had been ordered out from their camp to separate them from their women and children, and were formed about a hundred yards away, and Troops K and B were posted midway between them and their tepees. When ordered to surrender their arms they produced two broken carbines and stated that was all they had, but when the partial search of the tepee was made before the firing commenced, about forty arms were found, the *squaws* making every effort to conceal the same by hiding and sitting on them, and in various ways evidencing a most sullen mien. The disarmament was much more thorough than they expected, and when they found that the arms were to be taken from their *tepees* and those that they had concealed under their blankets were to be taken away also, they were carried away by the harangue of the ghost dancer, and, wheeling about, opened fire.

Most accounts claim that the vast majority of the Indians surrendered their arms willingly and only a few guns were found during a sweep of the tipis. The assertion that the hostilities began when the Indians wheeled about and opened fire was strongly denied by all non-military witnesses who offered that the struggle over a deaf Indian's firearm set off the shooting when it discharged.

Nothing illustrates the madness of their outbreak more forcibly than the fact that their first fire was so directed that every shot that did not hit a soldier must have gone through their own village. There is little doubt that the first killing, of women and children was by the first fire of the Indians themselves. They then made a rush to break through and around the flanks of Troop K, commanded by the gallant Capt. Wallace, and reached their *tepees*, where many of them had left their arms with the squaws and they continued the firing from among their own women and children . . . their women and children were mingled with them. The women and children were never away from the immediate company of the men after the latter broke from the circle. Many of them, men and women, got on their ponies, and it is impossible to distinguish buck from squaw at a distance when mounted. The men fired from among the women and children in their retreat.

The report Major Kent and Captain Baldwin gave to Proctor indicated that Indian women and children were the first to be struck down by fire from Miniconjou warriors. This was discounted by other witnesses.

Cautions were repeatedly given both by officers and noncommissioned officers not to shoot squaws or children, and men were cautioned individually that such and such Indians were squaws. The firing by the troops was entirely directed on the men in the circle and in a direction opposite from the tepees until the Indians, after their break, mingled with their women and children, thus exposing them to the fire of the troops, and as a consequence some were unavoidably killed and wounded, a fact which was universally regretted by the officers and men of the Seventh Cavalry. This unfortunate phase of the affair grew out of circumstances for which the Indians themselves were entirely responsible. Major Whitside emphatically declares that at least fifty shots were fired by the Indians before the troops returned the fire. Several special instances of humanity in the saving of women and children were noted.

Much of the killing of Indian men, women, and children was done following the retreat to the ravine, a fact that was not addressed in the report issued by Proctor. In addition, the contention that the first fifty shots fired that day were from Indian guns would seem preposterous when the accounts of other witnesses are taken into consideration.

That it resulted in the loss of the lives of many good soldiers and the wounding of many others, as almost the total destruction of the Indian warriors, was one of the inevitable consequences of such acts of insane desperation.

The bodies of an Indian woman and three children who had been shot down three miles from Wounded Knee were found some days after the battle and buried by Capt. Baldwin of the Fifth Infantry on the 21st day of January, but it does not appear that this killing had any connection with the fight at Wounded Knee, nor that Col. Forsyth is in any way responsible for it. Necessary orders will be given to insure a thorough investigation of the transaction and the prompt punishment of the criminals.

Many more Indian bodies were discovered far away from Wounded Knee, but that fact was either ignored by or never reported to the Secretary of War, although it is unlikely that the murders were not related to the violence at Wounded Knee.

Source Redfield Proctor. "Col. Forsyth exonerated; his action at Wounded Knee justified. Decision of Secretary Proctor on the investigation—the colonel restored to the command of his gallant regiment." *New York Times* (February 13, 1891): 6 [accessed January 2010]. http://query.nytimes.com/mem/archive-free/pdf?res=9A03E7DA1F3BE533A25750C1A9649C94609ED7CF

10. Nelson Miles, *Serving the Republic*

Few white men played a more significant role in U.S. government-Native American relations than General Nelson Miles. Miles was involved in carrying out government policies regarding the Plains Indians and directed the activities of the soldiers during the waning months of 1890, which led to the massacre at Wounded Knee. He was not directly involved in the tragedy, however. His actions and orders during that critical time indicated that he sincerely hoped to bring about a peaceful solution. He had gained a tremendous respect for the Sioux during his two decades of involvement with Indians, including his stint beginning in March 1869 as a commander of the Fifth U.S. Infantry at the age of 30. He directed campaigns against the Cheyenne, Comanche, Kiowa, and Arapaho in Texas in the mid-1870s before being promoted to Brigadier General in 1880. He took over command of the Department of the Missouri in 1885 and was promoted to Major General in April 1890.

It was at that time that Miles assumed control of the various Sioux reservations. The problems that ensued forced him to take command of military operations in December. His reputation was forever tarnished by the Wounded Knee massacre, but he expressed a deep appreciation and profound understanding of the Indian philosophy and way of life in later writings, including the following excerpt from his biography titled Serving the Republic, *which was published two decades after Wounded Knee.*

One can scarcely realize the impression we experienced in being out on the wild plains alone with nature. Knowing that there is a country to the north of you more than seven hundred miles to the Canadian boundary and thence northward to the arctic regions, unoccupied by civilized inhabitants, while to the south, an equal distance, to the Mexican frontier, this belt of country embracing a territory east of the Rocky Mountains of fully six hundred thousand square miles. This belt of country was occupied by the great tribes of Indians that had been driven there by warfare with the white race or removed by the government from the settled portions of our Eastern country, as well as by those who were natives of that vast territory. It was over that great belt of unbroken country that the Indians roamed with unmolested freedom, often making excursions north into the territory of Canada and far south of the Rio Grande into Mexico.

Before the Indians obtained firearms and horses they were comparatively harmless, dwelt in villages, and, in a rude way cultivated the grounds to some extent. In fact, the early campaigns of Miles Standish, Church, St. Clair, Mad Anthony Wayne, Harrison, Taylor, and others, were made for the destruction of the Indians' villages and fields, as much as against the Indians themselves. Equipped only with bow and spear, their lives were most laborious. To obtain food required endless toil. If they succeeded in taking the deer or other animals for food, the labor of carrying them, often long distances, to the lodge or camp was most difficult. When they obtained firearms, through the avarice of the white traders, the task of obtaining food was much easier, and when they secured horses from the Mexican and white people, about one hundred and twenty-five years ago, their mode of life was entirely changed. They became a nomadic people and roamed over a vast territory with freedom and independence. In fact, they became the most expert horsemen in the world, and their young men went on expeditions from their villages, sometimes being absent for twelve months at a time. They lived by the chase, and thereby become the most adroit, cunning, skillful hunters.

By the use of the skins of animals, the feathers of birds, grass, and leaves, they disguised themselves in the most artistic manner, so that by remaining motionless they would be unnoticed by approaching or passing game, or could stealthily get near the wildest before being discovered. In fact, it was the art of making themselves almost invisible. I have seen hunting or war parties in the summer or spring time, when the fields and trees were covered with rich verdure, with their horses and parts of their bodies painted green, and wearing green blankets, leggings, and moccasins. Later in the season, when the leaves were turning and the grass was dead, they would be mounted on dun or roan ponies and clad in covering of varied colors. In winter they would have snow-white ponies, white blankets, caps, leggings, moccasins—everything about them as white as the driven snow. The wild deer and buffalo gave them food, shelter and raiment. The flesh of these animals gave them abundance of wholesome food, the buffalo robes made them comfortable, and the soft, strong buckskin with their bead and porcupine work and decorations gave them a bright and picturesque appearance. Buffalo and elk hides furnished excellent lodges that were warm in winter, cool in summer, and healthful at all seasons of the year. Their wealth consisted of the herds of horses, their lodges, and the few appliances for camp-life.

Their religion was monotheistic—they worshiped the God of nature, and the Great Spirit was their omnipotent Jehovah. They were grateful for the abundance of the earth—the sunshine, air, water, all the blessings of nature—and believed that all should share them alike. For one to wish to monopolize any part of the earth was to them the manifestation of a grasping disposition. Often the men of the most influence and greatest popularity in the tribe were the poorest, or those who gave most to others.

Moving from one picturesque valley to another or from one pleasant camp to another was their agreeable occupation. They

were the most democratic people of the world. Their government was dictated by council, where reason and logic held
sway. The power of argument developed the best natural ora-
tors. Their illustrations were usually drawn from nature, and
most impressive. Our government often sent members of the
Cabinet, Senate, House of Representatives, and other prominent citizens to meet them in council, and these were usually
met by native talent of equal force and eloquence. Their songs
were legend of war and sentiment, and there was the
same romance in their lives—in fact, more than in the lives of
people living far remote from the enjoyment of the beauties of
nature. They believed that death was a long journey to the
happy hunting-ground, and they placed the bodies of their
departed with the richest paraphernalia, upon high scaffolds
or in the branches of trees, where, with the songs of birds and
the changes of the seasons, they slowly disappeared into the
atmosphere.

While the vast herds of buffalo, deer, elk, and antelope
remained, they were sure of food and raiment. They were, however, soon to be deprived of their abundant riches. The wave of
civilization was moving over the western horizon. Its onward
march was irresistible. No human hand could stay that rolling
tide of progress. The pale faces moved over every divide; they
cordelled or pushed their boats up every river. They entered every valley and swarmed over every plain. They traveled in wagons and prairie-schooners, on foot or horseback. Herding their
little bands and flocks of domestic stock, they built their homes
on every spot of ground that could be made productive.
One great cause of disaffection among the Indians was the
destruction of the vast herds of buffalo, which seemed like ruth-
less sacrifice.

Within a few years millions of buffalo were killed for their hides,
and thousands of white men, the best rifle-shots in the world,
were engaged in the business. The buffalo, like the Indian, was
in the pathway of civilization.

Source Miles, Nelson Appleton. *Serving the Republic*. New York:
Harper & Brothers Publishers, 1911. 112–116.

11. S.L.A. Marshall, *Crimsoned Prairie*

It seemed that for every surviving witness or participant at Wounded Knee, there was at least a mildly different interpretation of what occurred. Some stories, however, differ greatly, to the point in which a listener might find it hard to believe that they were being told by people who were actually there. In the days following the massacre, the explanations of the soldiers were quite different from those expressed by the surviving Indians and the majority of the white civilians who watched it unfold.

Time has also served to make the events of that late December day a bit cloudier. In most recent years, however, the vast majority of those who have written or spoken about the event have termed it a "massacre" rather than a "battle." But until the Dee Brown bestseller Bury My Heart at Wounded Knee *drew attention to the tragedy and to the state of Indian affairs at that time in the early 1970s, the mass media portrayed the Sioux as little more than savages and Americans were more likely to believe those who did not characterize the event as a massacre.*

The arguments on both sides have always revolved around the availability to and use of weapons by Miniconjou warriors. Those who classify the event as a massacre claim that nearly all the guns had been confiscated by the soldiers before that of deaf Indian Black Coyote discharged, signaling the start of hostilities. Though they concede that the Lakota had successfully hidden a few guns and were also using knives and other weapons, they offer that they were overwhelmed by the soldiers' mass of arms, including the rapid-fire Hotchkiss guns. Those who argue that it was a battle assert that the Indians had stashed away many weapons and had even pre-planned an attack on the soldiers. They contend that the Sioux were well-armed when the firing began and were endangering the lives of every Cavalry man.

Among those who believed the latter was a writer named S.L.A. Marshall, who crafted Crimsoned Prairie *at about the same time as* Bury My Heart at Wounded Knee *was written and attempted to dispel the writings of Brown and others who classified the tragedy as a massacre. His vivid description of Wounded Knee included the following:*

Once such a tragedy of violence and horror is unloosed, there is no telling where it may end. Armed men massed and suddenly panicked may not be held to account. Nigh mindless, they are wholly irrational in action.

So it is wholly vain that afterwards from their easy chairs historians and tacticians lament that all control became lost, that no one intervened to block the almost inevitable reaction, and having thus deplored, from that point move to apportion the blame between the sides. While as a human creature, man is rational and emotional, at the cutting edge he is animal, framed in the struggle for existence. In that unfathomable and terrible instant of unexpected change when his life is at stake, he responds to his most primitive instincts and becomes unaccountable.

. . . Without any order being called, the cavalrymen under direct attack either took to their heels or fired back. No officer was in position to stop them. None could have put himself there had he so chosen, so close were the sides joined, so deafening was the tumult. Rifles were exploding right in the faces of soldier and brave. This hand-to-hand trading of fire could hardly have lasted more than a minute. The point-blank carnage was grim and great.

Their magazines emptied, the Sioux came on with clubs and knives for the final death grapple. These weapons, too, had been concealed under the blankets. Should any further item in proof be needed that they had prepared not simply to defend themselves but to attack?

About the tracking down and killing of fleeing Indians, which he readily admitted occurred, Marshall wrote:

Rarely in such episodes does the heart take over when the brain is less than half functioning.

Source Marshall, S.L.A. *Crimsoned Prairie: The Indian Wars.* New York, N.Y.: DeCapo Press, 1972. 244–246.

12. Tim Giago's Account of the Wounded Knee Incident, 1973

Tim Giago was a small boy when his father worked as a clerk in the trading post at the Wounded Knee village. He remembered a couple named Agnes and Clive Gildersleeve who ran the store. It was the Gildersleeves who were taken hostage and that same store that was destroyed when the militant American Indian Movement heeded the call from some Pine Ridge Oglala to stage a siege at Wounded Knee.

Giago, an Oglala Lakota, was born, raised, and educated at Pine Ridge before forging a career as a writer. He often expressed in his writing views on Indian affairs and, in fact, is now the publisher of Native Sun Newsletter. *Gaigo asserts that the takeover at Wounded Knee was not favored by the majority of Oglala at Pine Ridge. But he has remained particularly angry over the treatment of the Gildersleeves, whom he reported in other writings have never fully recovered from the violence perpetrated by the protesters. Though he has defended protests and other actions in regard to the plight of the American Indian and particularly the Sioux in his writings, Gaigo has contended that the Wounded Knee siege of 1973 achieved nothing but heartache and needless deaths.*

He also offers that AIM leader Russell Means was not popular with most Pine Ridge Oglala, citing the fact that Means lost the Oglala Sioux Tribal presidency election against Dick Wilson, against whose policies the dissident Indians were protesting in 1973. Gaigo wrote the following in 2009:

Google "Agnes Gildersleeve" and read what Mrs. Gildersleeve and her family had to say about this big lie. Her article begins,

"When the AIM terrorists took over the Indian village of Wounded Knee in February 1973, they robbed Agnes and Clive Gildersleeve's Trading Post and held them hostage. Agnes was a 68-year-old Chippewa Indian; her husband was white."

She goes on to tell how she and her husband were threatened with death. . . . If the truth be known there were several thousand Oglala Lakota opposed to the takeover of Wounded Knee and the ensuing violence. Means would have you believe that if one was not for AIM then they were against them. It was politically astute for AIM to attempt dividing the Oglala people by creating a line between them that said "our side and their side." There were many sides to the Wounded Knee occupation and most of them did not approve.

. . . There were no winners at Wounded Knee 1973. Poverty is still rampant on the Pine Ridge Reservation and the unemployment rate is around 75 percent. Babies are still dying at birth at a rate far and above the national average and diabetes is epidemic.

Source Giago, Tim. No Winners at Wounded Knee 1973. Indianz.com, March 5, 2009 [accessed January 2010]. http://64.38.12.138/News/2009/013419.asp

13. A Modern Lakota's Look at the Future

Joseph M. Marshall III, who was raised on the Rosebud Sioux reservation before becoming a prominent author and actor, has written several books about Indian history and culture, focusing on the Lakota. Among his works is a biography of Crazy Horse. He served as a consultant and narrator for the 2005 TV miniseries titled Into the West.

A winner of the Wyoming Humanities Award, Marshall brings a positive outlook on the future of Native Americans to his writing, particularly in his book, The Day the World Ended at Little Bighorn. *His writing expresses pride over the Lakota victory at Little Bighorn, as well as his optimistic view that the spirit of his fellow Lakota will see them through the most difficult of times.*

The following excerpt from The Day the World Ended at Little Bighorn *captures his expectation of a brighter day.*

Since we Lakota are able to look back from the perspective of the twenty-first century, we are obviously not extinct as a people. We modern Lakota have not lived the buffalo-hunting lifestyle. As much as some, or perhaps many of us, know of it, we have not been there. We only know intellectually what was lost. We only know intellectually what our ancestors had to endure in order to adapt to a new lifestyle. But we should be fully aware that we are the manifestation of that change. We are here because our grandparents, great-grandparents, and great-great-grandparents faced and endured forced change with their strength: the virtues and beliefs that had sustained them as Lakota people. They endured the end of their world to ensure that there would be a Lakota nation to emerge from that trauma.

The Battle of the Little Bighorn was not the reason our world came to an end. But it did reaffirm for us that we were a strong nation quite capable of defending ourselves. We, and our Northern Cheyenne friends, were the victors at Little Bighorn. Non-Indian historians will admit that, but in the same breath remind us that we did lose the war. Among us there is a notion that the "war" is not over. Someday, perhaps, we will celebrate another victory, but not a victory won by fighting men with rifles and bows and arrows. Someday we will celebrate a victory of the spirit because the forces that sent armies to her our ancestors onto reservations could not destroy the essence of our culture.

Source Marshall, Joseph M. III. *The Day the World Ended at Little Big-horn*. New York: Penguin Group, 2007. 229–230.

Glossary

agencies U.S. government administrative groups that oversaw Indian affairs on reservations.

American Indian Movement (AIM) The American Indian civil rights movement launched in 1968 and greatly responsible for the Wounded Knee uprising of 1973.

Arapaho An Indian tribe that inhabited areas of Colorado and Wyoming, some of whom were killed in the Sand Creek Massacre of 1864.

artillery Large, powerful, mounted guns on wheels or tracks.

Badlands An area of southwest South Dakota and northwest North Dakota featuring colorful rock formations frequented by the Sioux.

Black Hills An area of South Dakota and Wyoming considered sacred hunting grounds by the Sioux Nation that was eventually lost to white miners and settlers following a discovery of gold in 1874.

Bluecoats A term used by the Sioux to describe those in the U.S. Cavalry.

Bozeman Trail A trail through Indian Territory connecting Montana with the Oregon Trail used by gold seekers and often the site of Indian attacks.

Brule A Teton Sioux tribe.

Buffalo Bill's Wild West Show A show headed by Buffalo Bill Cody featuring a wide variety of attractions in the 1880s that used Sioux chief Sitting Bull for one year to lure paying customers.

cavalry Soldiers on horseback used in military operations against American Indians during the nineteenth century.

Cheyenne An Indian tribe of the southwest divided into southern and northern bands that aided in the triumph at Little Bighorn and eventually placed on reservations.

commission A government-appointed group of people who discussed and took action to solve problems such as Indian relations.

Court of Inquiry A group that investigated the Wounded Knee Massacre and exonerated the cavalry and its leaders.

Cree A tribe with bands in the Plains that were often raided by bands of Lakota Sioux.

Crow A rival tribe to the Lakota Sioux, some of whom became Indian scouts that aided the government.

Dawes Act (or General Allotment Act) An 1887 act of Congress that individualized and redistributed reservation land inhabited by American Indians with the purpose of absorbing the tribes into the greater American society.

Divine Providence The notion embraced by some whites that God had provided North American lands for them.

extermination The eventual dying out of Indian people through disease, starvation, and warfare.

forts Fortified places occupied by American cavalry troops in various areas from which to plan and carry out military actions, sometimes against Indians, during the late 1800s.

ghost shirts Shirts bearing a variety of occult symbols sometimes worn by Indians performing the Ghost Dance in 1889 and 1890. The shirts were intended to prevent the Indians from being harmed by ammunition fired at them by government troops.

Great Father In Sioux terminology, the American president.

Great Spirit The god worshiped by the Plains Indians that had power over everything that existed and had deemed the Black Hills to be their sacred territory.

Hotchkiss gun   A rapid-firing cannon that played a role in subduing and killing Sioux during the Wounded Knee Massacre.

Hunkpapa   A Sioux tribe whose most famous and revered leaders were chief Sitting Bull and warrior Gall.

"Iron Horse"   A train, in Sioux terminology.

Lakota Sioux   A nation of Sioux tribes that includes the Brule, Hunkpapa, and Oglala.

Manifest Destiny   The theory of white superiority that deemed that white people were destined to dominate and control the North American continent.

medicine man   An Indian religious leader believed to possess supernatural healing powers.

Miniconjou   A Lakota Sioux tribe whose chief Big Foot played a key role in the events leading up to and including the Wounded Knee Massacre. The Miniconjou were the primary tribe involved in the massacre.

nomadic   In American Indian history, tribes that didn't remain in one place for long periods of time.

Oglala   A Lakota Sioux tribe known for chief Red Cloud, warrior Crazy Horse, and its role in the destruction of the Seventh Cavalry at Little Bighorn.

Pine Ridge   One of several reservations on which Sioux were placed in the late 1800s. Noted for its proximity to Wounded Knee, it was the reservation the Indians massacred at Wounded Knee had believed they were destined for.

Plains Indians   Indian nations including the Sioux, Cheyenne, Blackfoot, and Comanche that inhabited and hunted in areas from the Mississippi River to the Rocky Mountains and from the south to Mexico and north to Canada.

raids   An aggressive activity by Indian tribes to steal horses and other goods from neighboring tribes.

rations   Generally a limited amount of food and other necessities provided reservation Indians.

reservation   Lands given to or forced upon American Indians by the U.S. government beginning in the late 1860s.

Santee   A Sioux tribe most noted for their massacre of American citizens in Minnesota in 1862 and the subsequent mass hanging of their own people.

sovereignty   Independence in governing one's own affairs.

Standing Rock   One of several reservations on which Sioux were placed in the late 1800s. Most noted as the reservation on which Hunkpapa chief Sitting Bull was killed in 1890.

subjugation   To repress or keep down.

Sun Dance   A ceremony practiced by Indians to pay homage to the Great Spirit.

Wakan Tanka   The Great Spirit. A holy man.

Annotated Bibliography

Books

Bronson, Edgar B. *Reminiscences of a Ranchman*. New York: McClure Company, 1908.
http://books.google.com/books?id=YA8 TAAAAYAAJ&pg=PA167 &dq=Reminiscences+of+a+Ranchman:+%22Our+hearts+are+ sore+for+you%22#v=onepage&q=&f=false

> Not only does Bronson's first-hand account of the years fol-lowing the Battle of the Little Bighorn provide exciting read-ing, it gives an accurate view of the battles waged as officials attempted to rein in the Sioux and Cheyenne. Chapter 7, titled "A Finish Fight For a Birthright" describes the era from 1877 to 1881, after which the Indians had become more subdued on the reservations.

Eastman, Charles. *From the Deep Woods to Civilization*. Boston: Little, Brown and Company, 1916. 108–09. Reprinted by Dover Publications, 2003.
http://books.google.com/books?id=RG0_AAAAMAAJ&dq=charles +eastman+from+the+deep+woods+to+civilization&printsec= frontcover&source=bn&hl=en&ei=_ypiS-GwIpTCNdqM5MAP& sa=X&oi=book_result&ct=result&resnum=4&ved=0CBgQ6AEw Aw#v=onepage&q=&f=false

> This author was a Pine Ridge doctor and *Santee Sioux* who bore witness to many of the conflicts in the months leading up to the Wounded Knee Massacre, including the fear of white officials over the Ghost Dance. He used his medical skills following the tragedy and wrote with passion about the conflicts of a man with Indian blood living in white society af-ter three hundred of his *Sioux* brethren had been killed.

Lyman, Stanley. *Wounded Knee 1973: A Personal Account.* Lincoln, NB: University of Nebraska Press, 1993.

McLaughlin, James. *My Friend the Indian.* Boston and New York: Houghton Mifflin, 1910. 202–04.
http://books.google.com/books?id=YgYcAAAAMAAJ&dq=james
+mclaughlin:+my+friend+the+india&printsec=frontcover&
source=bl&ots=m_5RYE0fsJ&sig=FL3OndZDRlyTnP3RRew
4SRW988Q&hl=en&ei=jSOfSrTjO5PMMrnqwKoK&sa=X&oi=
book_result&ct=result&resnum=5#v=onepage&q=&f=false

> No white official came into greater conflict with *Hunkpapa* leader Sitting Bull than Standing Rock agent James McLaughlin. He wrote eloquently about his experiences with the revered chief and his own frustration over the inability to convince Sitting Bull to use his power to stop the spread of the Ghost Dance religion. His book tells the story of the attempted arrest of Sitting Bull that resulted in his death and began a chain reaction that led to the massacre at Wounded Knee.

Miles, Nelson. *Serving the Republic: Memoirs of the Civil and Military Life of Nelson A. Miles, Lieutenant-General, United States Army.* Cornell University Library, 2009. (First published 1911).
http://books.google.com/books?id=6QOOlln2HMsC&printsec
=frontcover&dq=Nelson+Miles:+Serving+the+Republic&
source=bl&ots=IDHKMItfsh&sig=_b4LMt4QgfxXquE617
FDGPIgFuI&hl=en&ei=PCtiS4etHZKKNI3u0OoL&sa=X&
oi=book_result&ct=result&resnum=1&ved=0CAcQ6AEwA
A#v=onepage&q=&f=false

> Miles played an integral role in the events leading up to the massacre at Wounded Knee and was a fascinating figure. He was involved in the subjugation of the *Lakota* on the reservations and though he chastised the Seventh Cavalry for their actions at Wounded Knee, his primary complaint was centered on their formation, which left some soldiers dead. But in this book, he wrote admiringly about the *Lakota* way of life when they were free people on the Plains.

Ostler, Jeffrey. *The Lakotas and the Black Hills: The Struggle for Sacred Ground*. New York: Viking Adult, 2010.

Richardson, Heather Cox. *Wounded Knee: Party Politics and the Road to an American Massacre*. New York: Basic Books, 2010.

Magazine Articles

Garland, Hamlin. "Two Moon's Story of the Battle: A Cheyenne's Account of the Battle of the Little Bighorn." *McClure's Magazine* 11 (1898): 444.
http://www.astonisher.com/archives/museum/two_moon_little_big_horn.html

> This article in one of the prestigious magazines of its time described the ordeal of Two Moon, whose Cheyenne helped give the Indians a tremendous numerical and military advantage at the Battle of the Little Bighorn. Two Moon was a participant in the destruction of the Seventh Cavalry as more of an outsider after the soldiers came upon the *Sioux* camp. Interestingly, the *Cheyenne* had been a rival of the *Lakota* earlier in the nineteenth century, but the Plains Indians banded together against the intrusion into their territory.

"The Indian Murderers in Minnesota." *Harper's Weekly*. (December 20, 1862): 807.
http://www.sonofthesouth.net/leefoundation/civil-war/1862/december/minnesota-sioux-massacre.htm

> *Harper's Weekly* was easily the most respected journal of the nineteenth century. In 1891 it published an account of an incident in which the frustrated and angry *Santee* massacred hundreds of Minnesotans because they had not received the rations they had been promised. The main thrust of this article was provided by a white citizen who visited the prison in which the arrested *Santee* were being held. The quoted gentleman spoke about his strong feelings against the Indians who perpetrated the killings. The article did not discuss the *Santee* perspective.

Newspaper Articles

Baum, L. Frank. *Aberdeen Saturday Pioneer.* (January 3, 1891). "L. Frank Baum's Editorials on the Sioux Nation: The Wounded Knee Editorial." [Accessed January 2010]. http://www.history.ox.ac.uk/hsmt/courses_reading/undergraduate/authority_of_nature/week_7/baum.pdf

> Perhaps the most perplexing philosophy about the state of Indian affairs was expressed by newspaper reporter L. Frank Baum, who gained far greater fame for authoring *The Wonderful Wizard of Oz*. Baum stated in this article that white leaders had treated the *Sioux* so badly for so many years that the best policy at that that point was the extermination of the Indians. He therefore claimed the massacre at Wounded Knee was justified.

"Confirmation of the Disaster." *New York Times.* (July 6, 1876). Little Bighorn Project: Newspaper Articles. [Accessed January 2009]. http://littlebighornproject.com/id31.html

> It took weeks for news of the Indian victory at Little Bighorn to hit the newspapers back east. When they were finally published, the accounts did not often offer an objective viewpoint. The Indians, whose numbers in the battle were exaggerated, were termed "Red Devils," though the basic account of the battle was accurate. General Custer was chastised for his reckless actions that left his troops vulnerable. This article provides a strong example of the biased reporting by journalists and military leaders of that era on battles between the cavalry and American Indians.

Proctor, Redfield. "Col. Forsyth exonerated; his action at Wounded Knee justified. Decision of Secretary Proctor on the investigation – the colonel restored to the command of his gallant regiment," *New York Times*, Page 6. February 13, 1891. http://query.nytimes.com/mem/archive-free/pdf?res=9A03E7DA 1F3BE533A25750C1A9649C94609ED7CF

> This *New York Times* article reports the Wounded Knee incident as told by participants from the Seventh Cavalry. Historians

have noted that the accounts from members of the cavalry are so similar that it is likely that they were told exactly what to say.

"The Great Chief: Red Cloud Meets His White Brethren at Cooper Institute." *New York Times* (June 17, 1870): 1. http://query.nytimes.com/mem/archive-free/pdf?_r=1&res=980 1E7DD1F3CE13BBC4F52DFB066838B669FDE

This sympathetic look at revered *Sioux* chief Red Cloud dem-onstrates that not all whites looked at Indians as savages. Red Cloud was received quite warmly by the audience in New York, particularly after he spoke humbly about the motivations of his people to enjoy the lifestyle to which they had become accustomed for generations. Other speakers, including a representative of the Indian Commission, pre-ceded him with utterances about the need to live peacefully with those who had occupied American lands for hundreds of years.

"The Last of Sitting Bull." *St. Louis Republic.* (December 17, 1890). First Nations. (Accessed January 2010). http://www.dickshovel.com/greasy.html

Though *Hunkpapa* chief Sitting Bull was revered by many Americans after having appeared with Buffalo Bill in the 1885 Wild West Show, his defiance and militancy had many applauding when he was killed in mid-December 1890. This editorial was written by an unnamed author whose hatred for Sitting Bull was pronounced.

Websites

Lakhota.com. http://www.lakhota.com/

EyeWitnesstohistory.com. Massacre at Wounded Knee, 1890. http://www.eyewitnesstohistory.com/knee.htm

Indigenouspeople.net. Sitting Bull. http://www.indigenouspeople.net/sittbull.htm

Films

HBO Home Video. 2007. *Bury My Heart at Wounded Knee.* http://www.amazon.com/Bury-My-Heartat-Wounded-Knee/dp/ B000R20164

Warner Home Video. 1995. *500 Nations.* http://www.amazon.com/gp/product/B0002S65WC/ref=pd_lpo _k2_dp_sr_2?pf_rd_p=486539851&pf_rd_s=lpo-top-stripe-1& pf_rd_t=201&pf_rd_i=B000R20164&pf_rd_m=ATVPDKIKX 0DER&pf_rd_r=0DCD6CNSGFJ54C5YBZKJ

Lillimar Pictures. 2008. *Sitting Bull: A Stone in My Heart.* http://www.amazon.com/dp/B001659HDE

Index

About the Author

MARTIN GITLIN is a freelance writer based in Cleveland. His published works include *Audrey Hepburn: A Biography* (Greenwood 2009), *The Ku Klux Klan: A Guide to An American Subculture* (Greenwood 2009), and *Diana, Princess of Wales: A Biography* (Greenwood 2008).

www.ingramcontent.com/pod-product-compliance
Lightning Source LLC
Chambersburg PA
CBHW070446100426
42812CB00004B/1216